Madama Butterfly
(English and Italian Edition)

BY GIAOCOMO PUCCINI,
ANTONIO ROSSI

Contents

Italian	English

Act I

A Japanese house, terrace and garden.
Below, in the background, the bay, the harbour and the town of Nagasaki.
The curtain rises.
[From the room at the back of the little house, Goro, with much bowing and scraping, leads in Pinkerton, and with much ostentation but still obsequiously, draws his attention to the details of the structure. Goro makes a partition slide out at the back, and explains its use to Pinkerton]
[They come forward a little on the terrace]

Italian	English
Pinkerton *[surprised at all he has seen, says to Goro:]* E soffitto... e pareti…	**Pinkerton** *[surprised at all he has seen, says to Goro:]* And the walls… And the ceiling…
Goro *[enjoying Pinkerton's surprise]* Vanno e vengono a prova a norma che vi giova nello stesso locale alternar nuovi aspetti ai consueti.	**Goro** *[enjoying Pinkerton's surprise]* They come and they go just to suit your pleasure in the same room varying new and old arrangements
Pinkerton *[looking around]* Il nido nuzïal dov'è?	**Pinkerton** *[looking around]* The marriage chamber Where is it?
Goro *[pointing in two directions]* Qui, o là... secondo...	**Goro** *[pointing in two directions]* Here, or there… according…
Pinkerton Anch'esso a doppio fondo! La sala?	**Pinkerton** It's a quite fantastic expedient! The hall?
Goro *[showing the terrace]* Ecco!	**Goro** *[showing the terrace]* Here!

Italian	English
Pinkerton *[amazed]* All'aperto?...	**Pinkerton** *[amazed]* In the open?...
Goro *[makes the partition slide out towards the terrace]* Un fianco scorre...	**Goro** *[makes the partition slide out towards the terrace]* The wall slides this way...
Pinkerton *[whilst Goro is making the partitions slide out]* Capisco!... capisco!... Un altro...	**Pinkerton** *[whilst Goro is making the partitions slide out]* I see! … I see!... Another…
Goro Scivola!	**Goro** It slides along!
Pinkerton E la dimora frivola...	**Pinkerton** So it is a wonderful dwelling…
Goro *[protesting]* Salda come una torre da terra, fino al tetto. *[invites Pinkerton to go down into the garden]*	**Goro** *[protesting]* Steady like a tower from the ground, to the roof *[invites Pinkerton to go down into the garden]*
Pinkerton È una casa a soffietto. *[Goro claps his hands loudly three times]* *[enter two men and a woman who humbly and slowly go down on their knees before Pinkerton]*	**Pinkerton** It's an accordion house. *[Goro claps his hands loudly three times]* *[enter two men and a woman who humbly and slowly go down on their knees before Pinkerton]*
Goro *[in rather nasal tones, pointing to them]* Questa è la cameriera che della vostra sposa *[fulsomely]* fu già serva amorosa. Il cuoco... il servitor. Son confusi del grande onore.	**Goro** *[in rather nasal tones, pointing to them]* Here is the maid who has served your wife *[fulsomely]* with dedication. The cook… The servant. They are overwhelmed by such a great honor.

Italian	English
Pinkerton [impatiently] I nomi?	**Pinkerton** [impatiently] Their names?
Goro [pointing to Suzuki] Miss Nuvola leggiera. [pointing to one servant] Raggio di sol nascente. [pointing to the other servant] Esala aromi.	**Goro** [pointing to Suzuki] Miss Light Cloud. [pointing to one servant] Ray of the rising Sun. [pointing to the other servant] Sweet-scented Exhalation.
Pinkerton Nomi di scherno o scherzo. Io li chiamerò: musi! [pointing to them one by one] Muso primo, secondo, e muso terzo.	**Pinkerton** These are scornful nicknames. I will call them: ragamuffins! [pointing to them one by one] First ragamuffin, the second, and the third one.
Suzuki [still on her knees, but grown bolder, raises her head] Sorride Vostro Onore? Il riso è frutto e fiore. Disse il savio Ocunama: dei crucci la trama smaglia il sorriso. Schiude alla perla il guscio, apre all'uomo l'uscio del Paradiso. Profumo degli Dei... Fontana della vita... Disse il savio Ocunama: dei crucci la trama smaglia il sorriso. [Pinkerton is bored, and his attention wanders]	**Suzuki** [still on her knees, but grown bolder, raises her head] Does Your Honor smile? A smile is like a fruit and a flower. Thus said the wise Ocunama: Every troubles a smile defies. A smile opens the shell to reach the pearl, opens the gates that led to Heaven. The perfume of the Gods... The Fountain of Life... Thus said the wise Ocunama: every troubles a smile defies. [Pinkerton is bored, and his attention wanders]
Goro [perceiving that Pinkerton begins to be bored at Suzuki's loquacity, claps his hands thrice]	**Goro** [perceiving that Pinkerton begins to be bored at Suzuki's loquacity, claps his hands thrice]

Italian	English
[The three rise and quickly disappear into the house]	*[The three rise and quickly disappear into the house]*
Pinkerton A chiacchiere costei mi par cosmopolita. *[to Goro who has gone to the back to look out]* Che guardi?	**Pinkerton** When they begin to talk women are all the same. *[to Goro who has gone to the back to look out]* What are you looking at?
Goro Se non giunge ancor la sposa.	**Goro** Watching if the bride is arriving.
Pinkerton Tutto è pronto?	**Pinkerton** Is everything ready?
Goro Ogni cosa. *[thanks with a deep bow]*	**Goro** Everything. *[thanks with a deep bow]*
Pinkerton Gran perla di sensale!	**Pinkerton** You are an admirable broker!
Goro Qui verran: l'Ufficiale del registro, i parenti, il vostro Console, la fidanzata. Qui si firma l'atto e il matrimonio è fatto.	**Goro** There will come: The Official Registrar, the relatives, your Consol, your fiancèe. Here you'll sign the contract and the marriage is done.
Pinkerton E son molti i parenti?	**Pinkerton** Are there many relatives?
Goro La suocera, la nonna, lo zio Bonzo (che non ci degnerà di sua presenza) e cugini, e le cugine... Mettiam fra gli ascendenti...	**Goro** Her mother, the grandmother, the uncle Bonzo (he won't honor us with his presence) male and female cousins... Let's count ancestors...

Italian	English
ed i collaterali, un due dozzine.	and other blood relations, around two dozens.
Quanto alla discendenza... provvederanno assai *[with obsequious presumption]* Vostra Grazia e la bella Butterfly.	As for descendants… they'll be looked after *[with obsequious presumption]* by Your Honor and the lovely Butterfly.
Pinkerton Gran perla di sensale! *[Goro thanks him with a deep bow]*	**Pinkerton** You are an admirable broker! *[Goro thanks him with a deep bow]*
Sharpless *[from within, rather far off]* E suda e arrampica! sbuffa, inciampica!	**Sharpless** *[from within, rather far off]* And sweating and climbing! Puffing, stumbling!
Goro *[who has run to the background, announces:]* Il Consol sale. *[bows low before the Consul]*	**Goro** *[who has run to the background, announces:]* Here comes the Consul. *[bows low before the Consul]*
Sharpless *[enters, quite out of breath]* Ah!... quei ciottoli mi hanno sfiaccato!	**Sharpless** *[enters, quite out of breath]* Ah!... Those pebbles have exhausted me!
Pinkerton *[goes to meet the Consul: they shake hands]* Bene arrivato.	**Pinkerton** *[goes to meet the Consul: they shake hands]* How good to see you.
Goro *[to the Consul]* Bene arrivato.	**Goro** *[to the Consul]* Welcome.
Sharpless Ouff!	**Sharpless** Ouff!
Pinkerton Presto Goro qualche ristoro. *[Goro hurries into the house]*	**Pinkerton** Quickly Goro some refreshment. *[Goro hurries into the house]*

Italian	English
Sharpless *[panting and looking around]* Alto.	**Sharpless** *[panting and looking around]* High up.
Pinkerton *[Pointing to the view]* Ma bello!	**Pinkerton** *[Pointing to the view]* But beautiful!
Sharpless *[looking at the sea and the town below]* Nagasaki, il mare, il porto...	**Sharpless** *[looking at the sea and the town below]* Nagasaki, the sea, the harbor…
Pinkerton *[pointing to the house]* e una casetta che obbedisce a bacchetta. *[Goro comes bustling out of the house, followed by the two servants. They bring glasses, bottles and two wicker lounges: they place the glasses and bottles on a small table, and return to the house]*	**Pinkerton** *[pointing to the house]* and this dwelling under the control of a magic wand. *[Goro comes bustling out of the house, followed by the two servants. They bring glasses, bottles and two wicker lounges: they place the glasses and bottles on a small table, and return to the house]*
Sharpless Vostra?	**Sharpless** Yours?
Pinkerton La comperai per novecentonovantanove anni, con facoltà, ogni mese, di rescindere i patti. Sono in questo paese elastici del par, case e contratti.	**Pinkerton** I bought this house for nine hundred and ninety nine years, but with the possibility, every month, to cancel the contract. In this curious country the houses and the contracts are elastic.
Sharpless E l'uomo esperto ne profitta.	**Sharpless** And a business man can profit from it.
Pinkerton Certo. *[invites Sharpless to be seated]*	**Pinkerton** Obviously. *[invites Sharpless to be seated]*

Italian	English
Pinkerton [*frankly*] Dovunque al mondo lo Yankee vagabondo si gode e traffica sprezzando rischi. Affonda l'áncora alla ventura... [*breaking off to offer Sharpless a drink*] Milk-Punch, o Wisky? [*resuming*] Affonda l'áncora alla ventura finchè una raffica scompigli nave e ormeggi, alberatura. La vita ei non appaga se non fa suo tesor i fiori d'ogni plaga,...	**Pinkerton** [*frankly*] All over the world the Yankee proud for pleasure and for business scorns every danger. He drops anchor for an unknown adventure... [*breaking off to offer Sharpless a drink*] Milk-Punch, or Wisky? [*resuming*] He drops anchor for adventure until a gust of wind upsets his ship, mooring and sail. He's not satisfied with his own life until he makes his treasures the flowers of every region.
Sharpless È un facile vangelo...	**Sharpless** That's an easy gospel to live by…
Pinkerton [*continuing*] d'ogni bella gli amor.	**Pinkerton** [*continuing*] and the love of every beautiful woman.
Sharpless è un facile vangelo che fa la vita vaga ma che intristisce il cor.	**Sharpless** That's an easy gospel that makes life delightful but that brings sadness to the heart.
Pinkerton Vinto si tuffa, la sorte racciuffa. Il suo talento fa in ogni dove. Così mi sposo all'uso giapponese per novecento novantanove anni. Salvo a prosciogliermi ogni mese.	**Pinkerton** Nothing can daunt him, no fate can crush him. His talent succeeds everywhere. So I'm marrying in Japanese way for nine hundred and ninety-nine years. With the option to annul the marriage every month.

Italian	English
Sharpless È un facile vangelo.	**Sharpless** That's an easy gospel.
Pinkerton ``America for ever!"	**Pinkerton** ``America for ever!"
Sharpless ``America for ever!"	**Sharpless** ``America for ever!"
Sharpless Ed è bella la sposa? *[Goro, who has overheard, approaches the terrace eagerly and officiously]*	**Sharpless** Is the bride pretty? *[Goro, who has overheard, approaches the terrace eagerly and officiously]*
Goro Una ghirlanda di fiori freschi. Una stella dai raggi d'oro. E per nulla: sol cento yen. *[to the Consul]* Se Vostra Grazia mi comanda ce n'ho un assortimento. *[The Consul laughingly declines]*	**Goro** Like a bouquet of budding flowers. A golden rays star. And for nothing: only one hundred yen. *[to the Consul]* If Your Grace commands me I can provide a fine selection. *[The Consul laughingly declines]*
Pinkerton *[very impatiently]* Va, conducila Goro. *[Goro runs to the back and disappears down the hill]*	**Pinkerton** *[very impatiently]* Go and fetch her, Goro. *[Goro runs to the back and disappears down the hill]*
Sharpless Quale smania vi prende! Sareste addirittura cotto?	**Sharpless** What hysteria has seized you! Are you really infatuated?
Pinkerton Non so!... non so! Dipende	**Pinkerton** I don't know!... I don't know! It depends

Italian	English
[rises impatiently, Sharpless rises also] dal grado di cottura! Amore o grillo, dir non saprei. Certo costei m'ha coll'ingenue arti invescato. Lieve qual tenue vetro soffiato alla statura, al portamento sembra figura da paravento. Ma dal suo lucido fondo di lacca come con subito moto si stacca, qual farfalletta svolazza e posa con tal grazietta silenzïosa, che di rincorrerla furor m'assale se pure infrangerne dovessi l'ale. **Sharpless** *[seriously and kindly]* Ier l'altro, il Consolato sen' venne a visitar! Io non la vidi, ma l'udii parlar. Di sua voce il mistero l'anima mi colpì. Certo quando è sincer l'amor parla così. Sarebbe gran peccato le lievi ali strappar e desolar forse un credulo cuor. **Pinkerton** Console mio garbato, quetatevi! Si sa, **Sharpless** Sarebbe gran peccato... **Pinkerton** la vostra età è di flebile umor.	*[rises impatiently, Sharpless rises also]* on the stage of infatuation! Love or a caprice, I can't tell you this. All I know is, she with her innocent charm has entrapped me. Fragile and delicate like crystal with her elegant figure, her posture she reminds me of a painting figure. But from her background of lacquer she suddenly detaches herself, and like a butterfly fluttering and settling with such silent elegance, that I'm seized by this madness to run after her even if I should break her wings. **Sharpless** *[seriously and kindly]* The other day, to the Consulate she came! I did not see her, but I heard her speak. And the mystery in her voice touched my soul. Surely a love that is pure speaks like that. It would be tragic to break those delicate wings and torture a heart full of love. **Pinkerton** My Dear Consul calm yourself! We know, **Sharpless** It would be a great shame… **Pinkerton** Men of your age care too much.

Italian	English
Non c'è gran male s'io vo' quell'ale drizzare ai dolci voli dell'amor!	There is no harm If I want those wings to guide to the sweet flights of love!
Sharpless Quella divina mite vocina non dovrebbe dar note di dolor!	**Sharpless** That divine and gentle voice should not sing about pain!
Pinkerton *[offers him more to drink]* Wisky?	**Pinkerton** *[offers him more to drink]* Wisky?
Sharpless Un'altro bicchiere. *[Pinkerton mixes Sharpless some whisky,* *and also fills up his own glass]*	**Sharpless** Bring me another. *[Pinkerton mixes Sharpless some whisky,* *and also fills up his own glass]*
Sharpless *[raises his glass]* Bevo alla vostra famiglia lontana.	**Sharpless** *[raises his glass]* Here's to your family far from here.
Pinkerton *[also raises his glass]* E al giorno in cui mi sposerò con vere nozze a una vera sposa... americana.	**Pinkerton** *[also raises his glass]* And to the day I will arrange a proper marriage to a real American... wife.
Goro *[reappears, running breathlessly* *up the hill]* Ecco! Son giunte al sommo del pendìo. *[pointing toward the path]* Già del femmmineo sciame qual di vento in fogliame s'ode il brusìo.	**Goro** *[reappears, running breathlessly* *up the hill]* There! They've just arrived at the top of the hill. *[pointing toward the path]* A crowd of women like the autumn leaves in the wind come bustling.
Butterfly's Girl Friends *(SA) [behind* *the scenes, far off]* Ah! ah! ah! *[Pinkerton and Sharpless retire to the*	**Butterfly's Girl Friends** *(SA) [behind* *the scenes, far off]* Ah! ah! ah! *[Pinkerton and Sharpless retire to the*

Italian	English
back of the garden, and look out at the path on the hillside]	*back of the garden, and look out at the path on the hillside]*
Girl Friends *(SA)* Ah! ah! ah! ah! ah! Quanto cielo! quanto mar! *[still within]* Quanto cielo! quanto mar!	**Girl Friends** *(SA)* Ah! ah! ah! ah! ah! So much sky! So much sea! *[still within]* So much sky! So much sea!
Butterfly *[within]* Ancora un passo or via.	**Butterfly** *[within]* Just one more step.
Girl Friends *(SA)* Come sei tarda!	**Girl Friends** *(SA)* How slow you are!
Butterfly Aspetta.	**Butterfly** Wait.
Girl Friends *(SA)* Ecco la vetta. Guarda, guarda quanti fior!	**Girl Friends** *(SA)* Here's the summit. Look, look so many flowers!
Butterfly *[serenely]* Spira sul mare e sulla terra	**Butterfly** *[serenely]* Blows across the sea and over the land
Girl Friends *(SA)* Quanto cielo! quanto mar!	**Girl Friends** *(SA)* So much sky! Su much sea!
Butterfly un primaveril soffio giocondo.	**Butterfly** A pleasant breeze of spring.
Sharpless O allegro cinguettar di gioventù!	**Sharpless** Oh happy chattering of youth!
Butterfly Io sono la fanciulla più lieta del Giappone, anzi del mondo. Amiche, io son venuta	**Butterfly** I am the happiest maiden in Japan, and in all world. Friends, I've arrived here

Italian	English
al richiamo d'amor d'amor venni alle soglie	to answer the call of love. I came to the love's threshold
Girl Friends *(SA)* Quanti fior! quanto mar! Quanto cielo! quanti fior! Gioia a te, gioia a te sia dolce amica,	**Girl Friends** *(SA)* So many flowers! So much sea! So much sky! So many flowers! Joy to you, joy to you sweet friend,
Butterfly ove s'accoglie il bene di chi vive e di chi muor.	**Butterfly** where is accepted the good of those who live and those who die.
Girl Friends *(S)* ma pria di varcar la soglia che t'attira volgiti e mira,	**Girl Friends** *(S)* But before crossing the threshold which attracts you turn around and look,
Girl Friends *(AA)* volgiti e mira le cose che ti son care,	**Girl Friends** *(AA)* turn around and loot at all the things that mean a lot to you,
Girl Friends *(SAA)* mira quanto cielo, quanti fiori, quanto mar!	**Girl Friends** *(SAA)* look at so much sky, so many flowers, so much sea!
Butterfly Amiche, io son venuta al richiamo d'amor, al richiamo d'amor, son venuta al richiamo d'amor!	**Butterfly** Friends, I come here at the call of love, at the call of love. I come here at the call of love!
Girl Friends *(S)* Gioia a te, gioia a te sia dolce amica, ma pria di varcar la soglia volgiti indietro e mira	**Girl Friends** *(S)* Joy to you, good luck to you. sweet friend, but before crossing the threshold turn around and look at

Italian	English
le cose tutte che ti son sì care!	all the things that mean a lot to you,
Girl Friends *(A)* Gioia a te, gioia a te sia dolce amica, ma pria di varcar la soglia volgiti indietro, dolce amica, e mira! *[Butterfly and her girl friends appear on the stage. They all carry large bright-colored sunshades open]*	**Girl Friends** *(A)* Joy to you, good luck to you. sweet friend, but before crossing the threshold turn around and look! *[Butterfly and her girl friends appear on the stage. They all carry large bright-colored sunshades open]*
Butterfly *[to her friends]* Siam giunte. *[sees the three men standing together and recognizes Pinkerton. She quickly closes her sunshade and at once introduces him to her friends]* F. B. Pinkerton. Giù. *[goes down on her knees]*	**Butterfly** *[to her friends]* We've arrived. *[sees the three men standing together and recognizes Pinkerton. She quickly closes her sunshade and at once introduces him to her friends]* F. B. Pinkerton. Down. *[goes down on her knees]*
Girl Friends *(SA)* *[close their sunshades and go down on their knees]* Giù. *[They all rise and ceremoniously approach Pinkerton]*	**Girl Friends** *(SA)* *[close their sunshades and go down on their knees]* Down. *[They all rise and ceremoniously approach Pinkerton]*
Butterfly Gran ventura.	**Butterfly** Great fortune.
Girl Friends *(S)* *[curtseying]* Riverenza.	**Girl Friends** *(S)* *[curtseying]* Our respect.
Pinkerton *[smiling]* È un po' dura la scalata?	**Pinkerton** *[smiling]* Was the climb a bit tiring?
Butterfly *[measuredly]* A una sposa	**Butterfly** *[measuredly]* To a well-mannered

Italian	English
costumata più penosa è l'impazienza...	bride is more tiring the impatience…
Pinkerton [*rather sarcastically, but not unkindly*] Molto raro complimento!	**Pinkerton** [*rather sarcastically, but not unkindly*] A very rare compliment !
Butterfly [*ingenuously*] Dei più belli ancor ne so.	**Butterfly** [*ingenuously*] Even better ones I could tell you.
Pinkerton Dei gioielli!	**Pinkerton** Jewels!
Butterfly [*anxious to show off her stock of compliments*] Se vi è caro sul momento...	**Butterfly** [*anxious to show off her stock of compliments*] If you care for some at present…
Pinkerton Grazie... no.	**Pinkerton** Thank you… no.
Sharpless [*after scanning the group of maidens with curiosity, approaches Butterfly, who listens to him attentively*] Miss Butterfly Bel nome, vi sta a meraviglia. Siete di Nagasaki?	**Sharpless** [*after scanning the group of maidens with curiosity, approaches Butterfly, who listens to him attentively*] Miss Butterfly Lovely name, it suits you so well. Are you from Nagasaki?
Butterfly Signor sì. Di famiglia assai prospera un tempo. [*to her friends*] Verità?	**Butterfly** Yes I am, sir. My family was once wealthy. [*to her friends*] Isn't that true?

Italian	English
Girl Friends (S) [assenting with alacrity] Verità!	**Girl Friends** (S) [assenting with alacrity] It is true.
Butterfly [quite simply] Nessuno si confessa mai nato in povertà, non c'è vagabondo che a sentirlo non sia di gran prosapia. Eppur conobbi la ricchezza. Ma il turbine rovescia le quercie più robuste... e abbiam fatto la ghescia per sostentarci. [to her friends] Vero?	**Butterfly** [quite simply] No one confesses to be born in poverty, There is no wanderer who doesn't tell his tale of noble ancestry. Yet I have known richness. But the gust cuts down even the strongest oaks... And we had to work as geishas to support ourselves. [to her friends] True?
Girl Friends (S) [corroborating her] Vero!	**Girl Friends** (S) [corroborating her] True!
Butterfly Non lo nascondo, nè m'adonto. [noticing that Sharpless smiles] Ridete? Perché?... Cose del mondo.	**Butterfly** I don't deny it, and I am not ashamed of it. [noticing that Sharpless smiles] You're laughing? Why?... This is how the world turns.
Pinkerton [has listened with interest and turns to Sharpless] (Con quel fare di bambola quando parla m'infiamma...)	**Pinkerton** [has listened with interest and turns to Sharpless] (With her innocent manner of speaking she sets my heart on fire...)
Sharpless [he also is interested in Butterfly's prattle, and continues to question her] E ci avete sorelle?	**Sharpless** [he also is interested in Butterfly's prattle, and continues to question her] Do you have any sisters?
Butterfly Non signore. Ho la mamma.	**Butterfly** None, sir. I have my mother.

Italian	English
Goro *[importantly]* Una nobile dama.	**Goro** *[importantly]* A highly regarded woman.
Butterfly Ma senza farle torto povera molto anch'essa.	**Butterfly** But despite not being her fault she's very poor indeed.
Sharpless E vostro padre?	**Sharpless** And what about your father?
Butterfly *[stops short in surprise, then answers very shortly]* Morto. *The friends hang their heads. Goro is embarassed. They all fans themselves nervously.*	**Butterfly** *[stops short in surprise, then answers very shortly]* He's dead. *The friends hang their heads. Goro is embarassed. They all fans themselves nervously.*
Butterfly *[to break the painful silence, Butterfly turns to Pinkerton]* Ma ho degli altri parenti: uno zio Bonzo.	**Butterfly** *[to break the painful silence, Butterfly turns to Pinkerton]* But I have other relatives here: my uncle Bonzo.
Pinkerton *[with exaggerated surprise]* Senti!	**Pinkerton** *[with exaggerated surprise]* Listen!
Girl Friends *(S)* Un mostro di sapienza.	**Girl Friends** *(S)* An impressive wise man.
Goro Un fiume d'eloquenza!	**Goro** A fountain of eloquence.
Pinkerton Grazia, grazia, mio Dio!	**Pinkerton** Thank you, thank you, my God!
Butterfly Ci ho ancora un'altro zio! Ma quello...	**Butterfly** There's still another uncle! But that one…

Italian	English
Girl Friends *(S)* Gran corbello!	**Girl Friends** *(S)* He's unworthy!
Butterfly *[Kind-heartedly trying to hush them up]* Ha un po' la testa a zonzo.	**Butterfly** *[Kind-heartedly trying to hush them up]* His head is up in the air.
Girl Friends *(S)* Perpetuo tavernaio.	**Girl Friends** *(S)* He spends his days in a tavern.
Pinkerton Capisco, un Bonzo e un gonzo. I due mi fanno il paio.	**Pinkerton** I see, a thinker and a drinker. Such a funny couple.
Butterfly *[mortified]* Ve ne rincresce?	**Butterfly** *[mortified]* Does it upset you?
Pinkerton Ohibò! Per quel che me ne fo! *[while Pinkerton is speaking with Butterfly, Goro leads Sharpless up to the friends and cerimoniously introduces some of them to the Consul.]*	**Pinkerton** It doesn't. It's not my business! *[while Pinkerton is speaking with Butterfly, Goro leads Sharpless up to the friends and cerimoniously introduces some of them to the Consul.]*
Sharpless *[returning to Butterfly]* Quant' anni avete?	**Sharpless** *[returning to Butterfly]* How old are you?
Butterfly *[with almost childish coquetry]* Indovinate.	**Butterfly** *[with almost childish coquetry]* Try to guess.
Sharpless Dieci.	**Sharpless** Ten years old.
Butterfly Crescete.	**Butterfly** Older.

Italian	English
Sharpless Venti.	**Sharpless** Twenty.
Butterfly Calate. Quindici netti, netti; *[slyly]* sono vecchia diggià.	**Butterfly** Now lower. Fifteen, exactly fifteen. *[slyly]* I'm already old.
Sharpless Quindici anni!	**Sharpless** Fifteen years old!
Pinkerton Quindici anni!	**Pinkerton** Fifteen years old!
Sharpless L'età dei giuochi...	**Sharpless** The age of toys…
Pinkerton e dei confetti.	**Pinkerton** and of marriage.
Pinkerton *[To Goro, who claps his hands, summoning the three servants, who come running out from the house]* Qua i tre musi. Servite ragni e mosche candite. *[Goro gives them the orders which he in his turn takes from Pinkerton]* Nidi al giulebbe e quale è licor più indigesto e più nauseabonda leccornìa della Nipponerìa. *[Goro signs to the servants to hurry into the house and to bring out everything]* *[Having received fresh orders from Pinkerton, Goro is jsut going into the house himself, when he perceives some*	**Pinkerton** *[To Goro, who claps his hands, summoning the three servants, who come running out from the house]* Call my ragamuffins. Serve them candied spiders and flies. *[Goro gives them the orders which he in his turn takes from Pinkerton]* Mint julep and even some special liquors along with the sweetest delicacy in Japan. *[Goro signs to the servants to hurry into the house and to bring out everything]* *[Having received fresh orders from Pinkerton, Goro is just going into the house himself, when he perceives some*

Italian	English
more people climbing the hill; he goes to look, then runs to announce the new arrivals to Pinkerton and Sharpless]	*more people climbing the hill; he goes to look, then runs to announce the new arrivals to Pinkerton and Sharpless]*
Goro *[announces importantly]* L'Imperial Commissario, l'Ufficiale del registro, i congiunti.	**Goro** *[announces importantly]* The Imperial Commissioner, the Official Registrar, the relatives.
Pinkerton Fate presto. *[Goro runs into the house]* *From the path in the background Butterfly's relations are seen climbing the hill and passing along: Butterfly and her friends go to meet them: deep bows and kowtowing: the relatiosn stare curiously at the two Americans.* *Pinkerton has taken Sharpless by the arm, and leading him to one side, laughingly makes him look at the quaint group of relations.* *The Imperial Commissioner and the official Registrar remain in the background.*	**Pinkerton** Hurry up. *[Goro runs into the house]* *From the path in the background Butterfly's relations are seen climbing the hill and passing along: Butterfly and her friends go to meet them: deep bows and kowtowing: the relatiosn stare curiously at the two Americans.* *Pinkerton has taken Sharpless by the arm, and leading him to one side, laughingly makes him look at the quaint group of relations.* *The Imperial Commissioner and the official Registrar remain in the background.*
Pinkerton Che burletta la sfilata della nova parentela, tolta in prestito, a mesata,	**Pinkerton** What a joke is the procession of my new relatives, part of this monthly contract.
Relations and friends (4 only) *(S) [to Butterfly]* Dov'è?	**Relations and friends (4 only)** *(S) [to Butterfly]* Where is he?
Relations and friends (4 only) *(TT) [to Butterfly]* Dov'è?	**Relations and friends (4 only)** *(TT) [to Butterfly]* Where is he?

Italian	English
Butterfly, Relations and friends (4 others) *(AA)* *[pointing to Pinkerton]* Eccolo là!	**Butterfly, Relations and friends (4 others)** *(AA)* *[pointing to Pinkerton]* There he is!
A Cousin Bello non è.	**A Cousin** He's not handsome.
Relations and friends (4 only) *(TT)* Bello non è. in verità, Bello non è.	**Relations and friends (4 only)** *(TT)* He's not handsome. really, He's not handsome.
Pinkerton Certo dietro a quella vela di ventaglio pavonazzo, la mia suocera si cela.	**Pinkerton** I'm sure that behind that enormous drape of peacock feathers my mother in law is hiding.
Butterfly *[offended]* Bello è così che non si può... sognar di più.	**Butterfly** *[offended]* He's more handsome than you could... ever dream.
Relations and friends (4 only) *(SS)* Mi pare un re!	**Relations and friends (4 only)** *(SS)* He seems a king to me!
(2 only) Vale un Perù.	**(2 only)** He's worth a lot.
Relations and friends (4 others) *(AA)* Vale un Perù.	**Relations and friends (4 others)** *(AA)* He's worth a lot.
(2 others) Mi pare un re!	**(2 others)** He seems a king to me!
The Mother *[with deep admiration]* Mi pare un re!	**The Mother** *[with deep admiration]* He seems a king to me!
Cousin *[to Butterfly]* Goro l'offrì	**Cousin** *[to Butterfly]* Goro even offered him

Italian	English
pur anco a me.	to me.
Butterfly *[contemptuously, to her Cousin]* Si,.. giusto tu!	**Butterfly** *[contemptuously, to her Cousin]* Yes… just to you!
Pinkerton *[pointing to Yakuside]* E quel coso da strapazzo è lo zio briaco e pazzo.	**Pinkerton** *[pointing to Yakuside]* And that despicable looking dull is the drunk and mad uncle.
Relations and friends (3 only & 3 only) *(ST) [to the Cousin]* Ecco, perché prescelta fu, vuol far con te la soprappiù	**Relations and friends (3 only & 3 only)** *(ST) [to the Cousin]* Then, this is why she was chosen, she looks down on you.
Relations and friends (3 others) *(AT)* La sua beltà già disfiorì.	**Relations and friends (3 others)** *(AT)* Her beauty is vanishing.
Relations and friends (3 others) *(T)* *[pitying Butterfly]* La sua beltà già disfiorì.	**Relations and friends (3 others)** *(T)* *[pitying Butterfly]* Her beauty is vanishing.
Relations and friends (3 only & 3 only) *(ST)* Divorzierà.	**Relations and friends (3 only & 3 only)** *(ST)* He'll divorce her.
Cousin, Relations and friends (3 others) *(A)* Spero di sì.	**Cousin, Relations and friends (3 others)** *(A)* I hope he will.
Relations and friends (3 only & 3 others) *(T)* Spero di sì.	**Relations and friends (3 only & 3 others)** *(T)* I hope he will.

Italian	English
Relations and friends (3 only & 3 others) *(SA)* La sua beltà già disfiorì.	**Relations and friends (3 only & 3 others)** *(SA)* Her beauty is vanishing.
Goro *[annoyed at the idle chatter, goes from one to another, entreating them to lower their voices]* Per carità tacete un po'.	**Goro** *[annoyed at the idle chatter, goes from one to another, entreating them to lower their voices]* For God's sake just be quiet.
Uncle Yakusidé *[staring at the servants who are bringing wines and liquors]* Vino ce n'è?	**Uncle Yakusidé** *[staring at the servants who are bringing wines and liquors]* Where is the wine?
The Mother *[leering, trying to keep out of sight]*, **the Aunt** Guardiamo un po'.	**The Mother** *[leering, trying to keep out of sight]*, **the Aunt** Let's look around.
Relations and friends (4 special ones) *(S) [with satisfaction, to Yakusidé]* Ne vidi già color di thè, color di thè e chermisì!	**Relations and friends (4 special ones)** *(S) [with satisfaction, to Yakusidé]* I've seen some some is like tea, some is like tea, some is red!
Relations and friends (4 others) *(AA)* *[looking pityingly at Butterfly]* La sua beltà già disfiorì, già disfiorì. Divorzierà.	**Relations and friends (4 others)** *(AA)* *[looking pityingly at Butterfly]* Her beauty is vanishing, is vanishing. He'll divorce her.
The Mother, the Aunt, Relations and friends (tutti) *(SSA) [falsetto]* Ah! hu!	**The Mother, the Aunt, Relations and friends (tutti)** *(SSA) [falsetto]* Ah! hu!

Italian	English
Relations and friends *(T) [in a nasal tone]* Ah! hu!	**Relations and friends** *(T) [in a nasal tone]* Ah! hu!
The Mother, the Aunt, Relations and friends *(SA)* ah! hu!	**The Mother, the Aunt, Relations and friends** *(SA)* ah! hu!
The Mother Mi pare un re! in verità bello è così che non si può sognar di più. Mi pare un re! Bello è così che non si può sognar di più, sognar di più. Mi pare un re! Vale un Perù. Mi pare un re!	**The Mother** He seems a king to me! He's more handsome than you could ever dream. He seems a king to me! He's more handsome than you could ever dream. He seems a king to me! He's worth a lot. He seems a king to me!
Cousin *[to Butterfly]* Goro l'offrì pur anco a me, ma s'ebbe un no! Bello non è in verità! Goro l'offrì pur anco a me, ma s'ebbe un no. In verità bello non è, in verità. Divorzierà. Spero di sì. Divorzierà!	**Cousin** *[to Butterfly]* Goro even offered him to me, but I declined! He's not handsome in truth! Goro even offered him to me, but I declined! In truth he's not handsome. He'll divorce her. I hope so. He'll divorce her!
Relations and friends *(S)* Bello non è, in verità, bello non è! bello non è, in verità! Goro l'offrì pur anco a me, ma s'ebbe un no. In verità bello non è, in verità. Divorzierà. Spero di sì. Divorzierà!	**Relations and friends** *(S)* In truth he's not handsome, he's not. He's not handsome in truth! Goro even offered him to me, but I declined. In truth he's not handsome. He'll divorce her. I hope so. He'll divorce her!

Italian	English
Relations and friends *(A)* Bello è così che non si può sognar di più! Mi pare un re! Vale un Perù! In verità è così bel che pare un re, in verità mi par un re, in verità. Divorzierà. Spero di sì. Divorzierà!	**Relations and friends** *(A)* He's more handsome than you could ever dream. He seems a king to me! He's worth a lot! He's so handsome he seems a king, In truth he seems a king to me. He'll divorce her. I hope so. He'll divorce her.
Uncle Yakusidé Vino ce n'è? Guardiamo un po', guardiamo un po'. Ne vidi già color di thè, e chermisi, color di thè. Vino ce n'è? Vediamo un po'!	**Uncle Yakusidé** Is there any wine? Let's look around, let's look around. I've seen some like tea, some like blood, and some like tea. Is there any wine? Let's look around!
Relations and friends *(T)* Bello non è, in verità, bello non è. Goro l'offrì pur anco a te, ma s'ebbe un no! ma s'ebbe un no! La sua beltà già disfiorì, già disfiorì. Divorzierà. Spero di sì. Divorzierà!	**Relations and friends** *(T)* In truth he's not handsome. Goro even offered him to me, but I declined! I declined! Her beauty is vanishing, is vanishing. He'll divorce her. I hope so. He'll divorce her!
The Aunt Vale un Perù. In verità bello è così che non si può sognar di più. Mi pare un re! Bello è così che non si può sognar di più, sognar di più. Mi pare un re! Vale un Perù. Mi pare un re!	**The Aunt** He's worth a lot. In truth he's more handsome than you could ever dream. He seems a king to me! He's more handsome than you could ever dream. He seems a king to me! He's worth a lot. He seems a king to me!
Butterfly *[to the Cousin]* Sì... giusto tu!	**Butterfly** *[to the Cousin]* Yes... good story!

Italian	English
Goro [tries again to stop their chatter, then he signs them to be silent]	**Goro** [tries again to stop their chatter, then he signs them to be silent]
Per carità	For God's sake
tacete un po'...	Be silent now…
Sch! sch! sch!	Sch! sch! sch!
Sharpless [to Pinkerton, aside]	**Sharpless** [to Pinkerton, aside]
O amico fortunato!	O my lucky friend!
[at signs from Goro the relations and guest crowd together in a bunch, but still chattering excitedly]	[at signs from Goro the relations and guest crowd together in a bunch, but still chattering excitedly]
Relations and friends and the Cousin (S)	**Relations and friends and the Cousin** (S)
Ei l'offrì pur anco a me!	He even offered him to me!
Relations and friends and the Mother (A)	**Relations and friends and the Mother** (A)
Egli è bel, mi pare un re!	He's handsome, he seems a king to me!
Pinkerton	**Pinkerton**
Sì, è vero, è un fiore, un fiore!	Yes, it's true, she's a flower, a flower!
Sharpless	**Sharpless**
O fortunato Pinkerton,	Oh lucky Pinkerton,
[meanwhile Goro has made the servants bring out some small tables on which are placed various cakes, sweetmeats, wines, liquors, and tea sets.]	[meanwhile Goro has made the servants bring out some small tables on which are placed various cakes, sweetmeats, wines, liquors, and tea sets.]
Relations and friends and the Cousin (S)	**Relations and friends and the Cousin** (S)
Ei l'offrì pur anco a me!	He even offered him to me!
Relations and friends and the Mother (A)	**Relations and friends and the Mother** (A)
Egli è bel, mi par un re!	He's handsome, he seems a king to me!

Italian	English
Pinkerton L'esotico suo odore	**Pinkerton** Her exotic fragrance
Sharpless che in sorte v'è toccato	**Sharpless** That fate has given to you
Relations and friends and the Cousin *(S)* Ma risposi non lo vo'!	**Relations and friends and the Cousin** *(S)* But I said no!
Relations and friends and the Mother *(A)* Non avrei risposto no!	**Relations and friends and the Mother** *(A)* I would not have said no!
Pinkerton m'ha il cervello sconvolto.	**Pinkerton** It has confused my brain.
Sharpless un fior pur or sbocciato! *[They then place on one side some* *cushions and a table, with writing* *materials,]*	**Sharpless** A flower just bloomed! *[They then place on one side some* *cushions and a table, with writing* *materials,]*
Relations and friends and the Cousin *(S)* e risposi no!	**Relations and friends and the Cousin** *(S)* And I said no!
Relations and friends and the Mother *(A)* non direi mai no!	**Relations and friends and the Mother** *(A)* I would not say no!
Sharpless Non più bella e d'assai fanciulla io vidi mai di questa Butterfly. E se a voi sembran scede il patto e la sua fede	**Sharpless** A more lovely maiden, I've never seen than Butterfly. If you see as pure madness the agreement and the faith

Italian	English
Relations and Friends *(S)* Senza tanto ricercar io ne trovo dei miglior, e gli dirò un bel no, e gli dirò di no, di no!	**Relations and Friends** *(S)* With just a little effort I can find better men, and I will say no! and I will say no, no!
Relations and Friends *(A)* No, mia cara, non mi par, | è davvero un gran signor, nè gli direi di no, nè mai direi di no, di no!	**Relations and Friends** *(A)* No my dear, you're wrong, he's truly handsome, I wouldn't have answered no, I would never say no, no!
Butterfly *[to her people]* Badate, attenti a me.	**Butterfly** *[to her people]* Please, pay attention to me.
Pinkerton Sì, è vero, è un fiore, un fiore, e in fede mia l'ho colto!	**Pinkerton** Yes it's true, she's a flower, a flower and in my faith I've gathered it.
Relations and Friends *(TT)* E divorzierà, e divorzierà, divorzierà!	**Relations and Friends** *(TT)* She'll be divorced, she'll be divorced, she'll be divorced!
Sharpless badate!... Ella ci crede. *[points to Butterfly]*	**Sharpless** Watch out! … She believes in it. *[points to Butterfly]*
Butterfly Mamma, vien qua. *[to the others]* Badate a me: attenti, orsù, *[spoken, in childish tones]* uno, due, tre e tutti giù. *[at a sign from Butterfly they all kowtow to Pinkerton and Sharpless]* *[Butterfly introduces her relations to*	**Butterfly** Mother, come here. *[to the others]* Listen to me: all of you listen, *[spoken, in childish tones]* one, two, three everyone bow. *[at a sign from Butterfly they all kowtow to Pinkerton and Sharpless]* *[Butterfly introduces her relations to*

Italian	English
Pinkerton, whilst the others note with marked satisfaction the liquors and sweetmeats which have been spread]	*Pinkerton, whilst the others note with marked satisfaction the liquors and sweetmeats which have been spread]*
Butterfly Mia madre.	**Butterfly** My mother.
Pinkerton Assai felice.	**Pinkerton** Glad to meet you.
The Mother Vostra Grazia ha lo splendor del giglio.	**The Mother** Your Grace shines as a lilium.
Butterfly Mia cugina e suo figlio.	**Butterfly** My cousin and her son.
Pinkerton *[giving the child a playful smack; the latter draws back timidly]* Ben piantato... promette...	**Pinkerton** *[giving the child a playful smack; the latter draws back timidly]* He's growing strong… Promising…
The Cousin *[bowing]* Eccellenza...	**The Cousin** *[bowing]* Your Augustness…
Butterfly Lo zio Yakusidé.	**Butterfly** My uncle Yakusidè.
Pinkerton È quello?.. *[laughing loudly]* Ah! ah!	**Pinkerton** Is that he? *[laughing loudly]* Ah! ah!
Relations and Friends *(SAT)* *[pushing Yakusidé forward]* Yakusidé... *[laughing]* Ah! ah!	**Relations and Friends** *(SAT)* *[pushing Yakusidé forward]* Yakusidé... *[laughing]* Ah! ah!
Yakusidé *[laughing]* Eh! eh! eh! eh! *[obsequiously, to Pinkerton]* Salute agli avi, gloriose gesta.	**Yakusidé** *[laughing]* Eh! eh! eh! eh! *[obsequiously, to Pinkerton]* May your ancestry live forever.

Italian	English
Relations and Friends (one half) *(ST)* *[to Pinkerton]* Buona vista ai tuoi occhi.	**Relations and Friends (one half)** *(ST)* *[to Pinkerton]* May the Heaven smile to your eyes.
Relations and Friends (the other half) *(ST)* Buona pianelle ai piedi.	**Relations and Friends (the other half)** *(ST)* May your path be full of flowers.
Yakusidé Salute agli avi, gloriose gesta.	**Yakusidé** May your ancestry live forever.
Pinkerton *[thanks them all, and to get rid of them shows them the delicacies spread out, then he turns to Sharpless again]* Dio, come son sciocchi! *[Goro accompanies the Consul, the Commissioner and the Registrar to the table with writing materials. The Consul examines the papers and gets the bond ready.]* *[Pinkerton approaches Butterfly.]*	**Pinkerton** *[thanks them all, and to get rid of them shows them the delicacies spread out, then he turns to Sharpless again]* How foolish they are, God! *[Goro accompanies the Consul, the Commissioner and the Registrar to the table with writing materials. The Consul examines the papers and gets the bond ready.]* *[Pinkerton approaches Butterfly.]*
Pinkerton *[gently, offering Butterfly some sweetmeats, while the Mother and the Cousin rise and join the rest of the relatives]* All'amor mio! *[seeing that Butterfly appears embarrased]* Vi spiacciono i confetti?	**Pinkerton** *[gently, offering Butterfly some sweetmeats, while the Mother and the Cousin rise and join the rest of the relatives]* To my beloved bride! *[seeing that Butterfly appears embarrased]* Don't you like the sweetmeats?
Butterfly Signor B. F. Pinkerton, *[shows him her hands and arms which are encumbered by stuffed-out sleeves]* perdono... Io vorrei... pochi oggetti	**Butterfly** Mister B.F. Pinkerton, *[shows him her hands and arms which are encumbered by stuffed-out sleeves]* Forgive me... I'd like... just a few

Italian	English
da donna...	things for a woman…
Pinkerton Dove sono?	**Pinkerton** Where I can find them?
Butterfly [pointing to her sleeves] Sono qui... vi dispiace?	**Butterfly** [pointing to her sleeves] Here… Are you angry?
Pinkerton [rather astonished, smiles, then quickly and gallantly reassures her] O perché mai, mia bella Butterfly?	**Pinkerton** [rather astonished, smiles, then quickly and gallantly reassures her] Oh why, my lovely Butterfly?
Butterfly [empties her sleeves, placing their contents one by one on a stool] Fazzoletti. La pipa. Una cintura. Un piccolo fermaglio. Uno specchio. Un ventaglio.	**Butterfly** [empties her sleeves, placing their contents one by one on a stool] Handkerchiefs. A pipe. A belt. A little hair clip. A mirror. A fan.
Pinkerton [sees a jar] Quel barattolo?	**Pinkerton** [sees a jar] And that jar?
Butterfly Un vaso di tintura.	**Butterfly** A jar of carmine.
Pinkerton Ohibò!	**Pinkerton** Oh!
Butterfly Vi spiace?... [throws away the pot of paint] Via! [draws forth a long narrow sheath]	**Butterfly** Do you mind it? [throws away the pot of paint] Not at all! [draws forth a long narrow sheath]
Pinkerton E quello?	**Pinkerton** And that?

Italian	English
Butterfly [very gravely] Cosa sacra e mia.	**Butterfly** [very gravely] It's invaluable to me.
Pinkerton [curiously] E non si può vedere?	**Pinkerton** [curiously] And can I give a look?
Butterfly C'è troppa gente. [beseechingly and grave, lays down the sheath very reverently] Perdonate.	**Butterfly** Too crowd. [beseechingly and grave, lays down the sheath very reverently] Forgive me.
Goro [who has approached, whispers to Pinkerton] È un presente del Mikado a suo padre... coll'invito... [imitating the action of suicide]	**Goro** [who has approached, whispers to Pinkerton] It's a gift from the Mikado to her father… With a message... [imitating the action of suicide]
Pinkerton [softly to Goro] E... suo padre?	**Pinkerton** [softly to Goro] And … Her father?
Goro Ha obbedito. [withdraws, mingling with the guests]	**Goro** He obeyed. [withdraws, mingling with the guests]
Butterfly [takes some images from her sleeves and shows them to Pinkerton] Gli Ottokè.	**Butterfly** [takes some images from her sleeves and shows them to Pinkerton] The Ottokè
Pinkerton [takes one and examines it with curiosity] Quei pupazzi? Avete detto?..	**Pinkerton** [takes one and examines it with curiosity] Those puppets? What are they?
Butterfly Son l'anime degli avi. [puts down the images, then rises]	**Butterfly** They're the souls of my ancestry. [puts down the images, then rises]

Italian	English
Pinkerton Ah!... il mio rispetto.	**Pinkerton** Ah! … My respects.
Butterfly [leads Pinkerton to one side and says to him in respectfully confidential tones:] Ieri son salita tutta sola in secreto alla Missione. Colla nuova mia vita posso adottare nuova religione. [timidly] Lo zio Bonzo nol sa, nè i miei lo sanno. Io seguo il mio destino e piena d'umiltà al Dio del signor Pinkerton m'inchino. È mio destino. Per me spendeste cento yen, ma vivrò con molta economia. E per farvi contento potrò quasi obliar la gente mia. [goes to take up the images] E questi: via. [cutting short the note, and appearing alarmed lest her relatives should have overheard her] [Butterfly throws down the Ottoké]	**Butterfly** [leads Pinkerton to one side and says to him in respectfully confidential tones:] Yesterday I went alone and secretly to the Mission. To start my new life and to adopt a new religion. [timidly] My uncle Bonzo doesn't know it, not even my family knows it. I follow my own fate and humbly I'll bow to the God of Mister Pinkerton. This is my fate. For me you spent a hundred a yen, but I'll live a frugal life. And to make you happy I will forget my ancestry. [goes to take up the images] Then they disappear. [cutting short the note, and appearing alarmed lest her relatives should have overheard her] [Butterfly throws down the Ottoké]
Goro [Meanwhile Goro has approached the Consul, and having received his orders, thunders forth in stentorian tones:] Tutti zitti! [The chattering ceases: they all leave off eating and drinking and come forward in a circle, listening with much interest. Pinkerton and Butterfly stand in the centre.]	**Goro** [Meanwhile Goro has approached the Consul, and having received his orders, thunders forth in stentorian tones:] Silence now! [The chattering ceases: they all leave off eating and drinking and come forward in a circle, listening with much interest. Pinkerton and Butterfly stand in the centre.]

Italian	English
The Commissioner [reads out] È concesso al nominato Mister B. F. Pinkerton, Luogotenente nella cannoniera *Lincoln,* marina degli Stati Uniti America del Nord: ed alla damigella Butterfly del quartiere d'Omara-Nagasaki, d'unirsi in matrimonio, per dritto il primo, della propria volontà, ed ella per consenso dei parenti *[hands the bond for signature]* qui testimonî all'atto.	**The Commissioner** [reads out] I do decree Mister B.F. Pinkerton Lieutenant on the gunboat *Lincoln,* of the United States navy of North America: and to the maiden known as Butterfly from the district of Omara-Nagasaki, to be united in marriage, acting the former, of his accord and will, and the latter with the consent of her relatives *[hands the bond for signature]* here to witness the marriage.
Goro [with much unction] Lo sposo. *[Pinkerton signs]* Poi la sposa. *[Butterfly signs]* E tutto è fatto. *[The relatives hasten to sign]* *[The friends approach Butterfly full of congratulations and deep bows]*	**Goro** [with much unction] The bridegroom. *[Pinkerton signs]* Then the bride. *[Butterfly signs]* And all is done *[The relatives hasten to sign]* *[The friends approach Butterfly full of congratulations and deep bows]*
Girl Friends (S) Madama Butterfly.	**Girl Friends** (S) Madama Butterfly.
Butterfly [corrects them, with finger raised] Madama B. F. Pinkerton. *[The friends cluster round Butterfly and congratulate her: meanwhile the Registrar removes the bond and the other papers, then informs the Commissioner that the ceremony is over.]*	**Butterfly** [corrects them, with finger raised] Madama B. F. Pinkerton. *[The friends cluster round Butterfly and congratulate her: meanwhile the Registrar removes the bond and the other papers, then informs the Commissioner that the ceremony is over.]*

Italian	English
The Commissioner [congratulating Pinkerton] Augurî molti.	**The Commissioner** [congratulating Pinkerton] Congratulations.
Pinkerton I miei ringraziamenti. [bowing to him]	**Pinkerton** My sincere thanks. [bowing to him]
The Commissioner [approaches the Consul] Il signor Console scende?	**The Commissioner** [approaches the Consul] Mr. Consul, are you going away?
Sharpless L'accompagno. [nodding to Pinkerton] Ci vedrem domani. [shaking hands with Pinkerton]	**Sharpless** I'll go with you. [nodding to Pinkerton] We'll meet tomorrow. [shaking hands with Pinkerton]
Pinkerton A meraviglia.	**Pinkerton** Wonderful.
The Registrar [Taking leave of Pinkerton] Posterità.	**The Registrar** [Taking leave of Pinkerton] Best descendants to you.
Pinkerton Mi proverò. [The Consul, the Commissioner and the Registrar depart, to go down to the town]	**Pinkerton** I'll try my best. [The Consul, the Commissioner and the Registrar depart, to go down to the town]
Sharpless [Comes back again and says to Pinkerton in significant tones] Giudizio! [Pinkerton reassures him with a gesture and gives him a friendly wave of the hand] [Sharpless goes down by the path.	**Sharpless** [Comes back again and says to Pinkerton in significant tones] Be careful! [Pinkerton reassures him with a gesture and gives him a friendly wave of the hand] [Sharpless goes down by the path.

Italian	English
Pinkerton who has gone towards the background, waves his hand to him again.]	*Pinkerton who has gone towards the background, waves his hand to him again.]*
Pinkerton *[Returns to the front, and says to himself, rubbing his hands:]* (Ed eccoci in famiglia. Sbrighiamoci al più presto e in modo onesto.) *[gaily to Yakusidé]* Qua, signor Zio. *[mixing him some whisky]* Ah, ah, il bicchiere della staffa.	**Pinkerton** *[Returns to the front, and says to himself, rubbing his hands:]* (And now we are a family. Now let's free ourselves from them quickly and with honesty.) *[gaily to Yakusidé]* This way, uncle. *[mixing him some whisky]* Ah, ah, for you the stirrup cup.
Yakusidé Magari due dozzine!	**Yakusidé** Even better twenty!
Pinkerton *[giving him the bottle]* E allora la caraffa.	**Pinkerton** *[giving him the bottle]* Then the whole bottle.
Friends (some) *(T)* *[making fun of Yakusidé]* Il beone!	**Friends (some)** *(T)* *[making fun of Yakusidé]* The drunkard!
Friends (others) *(T)* Il beone!	**Friends (others)** *(T)* The drunkard!
Relations and Friends (some) *(S)* *[making fun of Yakusidé]* Il beone!	**Relations and Friends (some)** *(S)* *[making fun of Yakusidé]* The drunkard!
Relations and Friends (others) *(A)* Il beone!	**Relations and Friends (others)** *(A)* The drunkard!
Relations and Friends (some) *(T)* *[laughing]* Ah, ah, ah!	**Relations and Friends (some)** *(T)* *[laughing]* Ah, ah, ah!

Italian	English
Relations and Friends (S) [laughing] Ah, ah, ah!	**Relations and Friends** (S) [laughing] Ah, ah, ah!
Relations and Friends (others) (T) Ah, ah, ah!	**Relations and Friends (others)** (T) Ah, ah, ah!
Relations and Friends (A) [laughing] Ah, ah, ah!	**Relations and Friends** (A) [laughing] Ah, ah, ah!
Yakusidé [pompously, without heeding the mockers] Bevi il tuo Saki e a Dio piega il ginocchio.	**Yakusidé** [pompously, without heeding the mockers] Drink up your Saki and bow before the God.
Relations and Friends (S) [mocking him] Bevi il tuo Saki, bevi il tuo Saki e a Dio piega il ginocchio!	**Relations and Friends** (S) [mocking him] Drink up your Saki, drink up your Saki a bow before the God!
Relations and Friends (T) Bevi il tuo Saki, bevi il tuo Saki e a Dio piega il ginocchio.	**Relations and Friends** (T) Drink up your Saki, drink up your Saki and bow before the God.
Pinkerton [is about to mix some drink for Butterfly's mother] La suocera...	**Pinkerton** [is about to mix some drink for Butterfly's mother] For your mother…
Butterfly [stops him pouring out] Non beve.	**Butterfly** [stops him pouring out] She doesn't drink.
Pinkerton [turning from one to another and offering] Le cugine, le amiche,... due confetti e un bicchier di Porto.	**Pinkerton** [turning from one to another and offering] For your cousins, your friends, … some sweets and a cup of Porto.

Italian	English
Yakusidé *[coming forward eagerly]* Con piacere!	**Yakusidé** *[coming forward eagerly]* With pleasure!
Relations and Friends (half) *(S)* *[drive Yakusidé away]* Il beone!	**Relations and Friends (half)** *(S)* *[drive Yakusidé away]* The drunkard!
Relations and Friends (the other half) *(A)* Il beone!	**Relations and Friends (the other half)** *(A)* The drunkard!
Goro *[to Pinkerton, so that he may not encourage the drunkard too much]* Piano, signore, signore, piano! ch'egli berrebbe il gran padre oceàno!	**Goro** *[to Pinkerton, so that he may not encourage the drunkard too much]* Slowly, ladies, slowly, ladies! He could drink up even the ocean!
Relations and Friends *(STT)* Piano, signore, signore, piano! ch'egli berrebbe il gran padre oceàno!	**Relations and Friends** *(STT)* Slowly, ladies, slowly, ladies! He could drink up even the ocean!
Pinkerton *[to the child, giving him a lot of sweets]* A te marmocchio; spalanca le tue maniche e insacca, insacca chicche e pasticci a macca. *[takes a glass and raises it]* Ip! Ip!	**Pinkerton** *[to the child, giving him a lot of sweets]* To you, cherub; open up your hands and fill your sleeves with cakes and lots of sweets. *[takes a glass and raises it]* Ip! Ip!
Chorus *(S)* *[toasting]* O Kami! o Kami!	**Chorus** *(S)* *[toasting]* O Kami! o Kami!
Pinkerton Beviamo ai novissimi legami,	**Pinkerton** A toast to the new bonds,
Yakusidé, Chorus *(T)* O Kami! o Kami!	**Yakusidé, Chorus** *(T)* O Kami! o Kami!

Italian	English
Pinkerton beviamo ai novissimi legami.	**Pinkerton** A toast to the new bonds.
Cousin, The Mother Beviamo, beviamo!	**Cousin, The Mother** Let's drink, let's drink!
a Cousin, The Mother, Chorus *(SA)* O Kami! o Kami! Beviamo ai novissimi legami. *[the toasts are interrupted by strange cries coming from the path on the hill]*	**a Cousin, The Mother, Chorus** *(SA)* O Kami! o Kami! A toast to the new bonds. *[the toasts are interrupted by strange cries coming from the path on the hill]*
Her uncle, the Bonze *[from the distance]* Cio-cio-san! *[at this shout all the relations and friends are thunderstruck, and huddle together in terror: Butterfly remains alone in a corner]* Cio-cio-san! Abbominazione!	**Her uncle, the Bonze** *[from the distance]* Cho-cho-san! *[at this shout all the relations and friends are thunderstruck, and huddle together in terror: Butterfly remains alone in a corner]* Cho-cho-san! Abomination!
Butterfly, Chorus *(ST)* *[amazed]* Lo zio Bonzo!	**Butterfly, Chorus** *(ST)* *[amazed]* It's uncle Bonzo!
Goro *[annoyed at the Bonze's arrival]* Un corno al guastafeste! Chi ci leva d'intorno le persone moleste?...	**Goro** *[annoyed at the Bonze's arrival]* A curse on this killjoy! Who can take away this troublemaker?
The Bonze Cio-cio-san! Cio-cio-san!	**The Bonze** Cho-cho-san!Cho-cho-san!
Goro *[signs to the servants to take away the tables, stools and cushions; and then prudently retires, grumbling furiously]*	**Goro** *[signs to the servants to take away the tables, stools and cushions; and then prudently retires, grumbling furiously]*

Italian	English
The Bonze [coming nearer] Cio-cio-san! [In the background appears the odd figure of the Bonze, who comes forward in a rage] Cio-cio-san!	**The Bonze** [coming nearer] Cho-cho-san! [In the background appears the odd figure of the Bonze, who comes forward in a rage] Cho-cho-san!
The Bonze [at the sight of Butterfly, who stands isolated from the rest, the Bonze stretches out his hands threateningly towards her] Che hai tu fatto alla Missione?	**The Bonze** [at the sight of Butterfly, who stands isolated from the rest, the Bonze stretches out his hands threateningly towards her] Why did you go to the Mission?
Chorus and the Cousin (ST) Rispondi, Cio-cio-san!	**Chorus and the Cousin** (ST) Answer him, Cho-cho-san!
Pinkerton [angry at the scene made by the Bonze] Che mi strilla quel matto?	**Pinkerton** [angry at the scene made by the Bonze] What's the lunatic yelling?
The Bonze Rispondi, che hai tu fatto?	**The Bonze** Give answer, what were you doing?
Friends and relations (ST) [anxiously, turning to Butterfly] Rispondi, Cio-cio-san!	**Friends and relations** (ST) [anxiously, turning to Butterfly] Answer him, Cho-cho-san!
The Bonze Come, hai tu gli occhi asciutti? Son dunque questi i frutti? [shouting] Ci ha rinnegato tutti!	**The Bonze** How then, are your eyes dry? Are these the fruits of evil? [shouting] She has renounced our family!
Chorus (SATT) [scandolized, shouting long and loud] Hou! Cio-cio-san!	**Chorus** (SATT) [scandolized, shouting long and loud] Hou! Cho-cho-san!

Italian	English
The Bonze Rinnegato vi dico,... il culto antico.	**The Bonze** She has renounced, let me tell you, our ancient religion.
Chorus *(ST) [shouting]* Hou! Cio-cio-san!	**Chorus** *(ST) [shouting]* Hou!Cho-cho-san!
The Bonze *[hurls imprecations at Butterfly, who hides her face in her hands: her mother comes forward to protect her, but the Bonze pushes her away roughly, and approaches Butterfly in a fury, shouting in her face:]* Kami sarundasico!	**The Bonze** *[hurls imprecations at Butterfly, who hides her face in her hands: her mother comes forward to protect her, but the Bonze pushes her away roughly, and approaches Butterfly in a fury, shouting in her face:]* Kami sarundasico!
Chorus *(ST)* Hou! Cio-cio-san!	**Chorus** *(ST)* Hou!Cho-cho-san!
The Bonze All'anima tua guasta qual supplizio sovrasta!	**The Bonze** May your lost soul be tormented!
Pinkerton *[has lost patience, and intervenes between the Bonze and Butterfly]* Ehi, dico: basta, basta!	**Pinkerton** *[has lost patience, and intervenes between the Bonze and Butterfly]* Hei, I say: that's enough, enough!
The Bonze *[at the sound of Pinkerton's voice the Bonze stops short in amazement, then with a sudden resolve he invites relations and friends to come away]* Venite tutti. Andiamo! *[to Butterfly]* Ci hai rinnegato e noi... *[all retire hastily to the back and stretch their arms towards Butterfly]*	**The Bonze** *[at the sound of Pinkerton's voice the Bonze stops short in amazement, then with a sudden resolve he invites relations and friends to come away]* All leave her. Come with me! *[to Butterfly]* You renounced us and we… *[all retire hastily to the back and stretch their arms towards Butterfly]*

Italian	English
Yakusidé and The Bonze, Chorus and Cousin *(ST)* Ti rinneghiamo!	**Yakusidé and The Bonze, Chorus and Cousin** *(ST)* renounced you!
Pinkerton *[authoritatively ordering all to depart]* Sbarazzate all'istante. In casa mia niente baccano e niente bonzeria.	**Pinkerton** *[authoritatively ordering all to depart]* Now leave this place! No noise and babel in my house.
Chorus *(ST) [shout]* Hou! *[at Pinkerton's words, they all rush hastily towards the path which leads down to the town: Butterfly's mother again tries to approach her, but is dragged away by the others]*	**Chorus** *(ST) [shout]* Hou! *[at Pinkerton's words, they all rush hastily towards the path which leads down to the town: Butterfly's mother again tries to approach her, but is dragged away by the others]*
Chorus *(ST) [as they go out]* Hou! Cio-cio-san! *[rather far off]* Hou! Cio-cio-san! *[By degrees the voices grow faint in the distance.Butterfly remains motionless and silent, her face buried in her hands, whilst Pinkerton has gone to the top of the path, to make sure that all these troublesome guest have really gone]*	**Chorus** *(ST) [as they go out]* Hou! Cho-cho-san! *[rather far off]* Hou! Cho-cho-san! *[By degrees the voices grow faint in the distance.Butterfly remains motionless and silent, her face buried in her hands, whilst Pinkerton has gone to the top of the path, to make sure that all these troublesome guest have really gone]*
The Bonze, Yakusidé, Chorus *(T)* Kami sarundasico	**The Bonze, Yakusidé, Chorus** *(T)* Kami sarundasico
Chorus *(S)* Hou! Cio-cio-san!	**Chorus** *(S)* Hou! Cho-cho-san!
The Bonze, Yakusidé, Chorus *(T)* Ti rinneghiamo!	**The Bonze, Yakusidé, Chorus** *(T)* We renounced you!

Italian	English
Relations and friends *(S)* *[emphatically]* Hou! Cio-cio-san!	**Relations and friends** *(S)* *[emphatically]* Hou!Cho-cho-san!
The Bonze, Yakusidé, Chorus *(ST)* *[emphatically]* Ti rinneghiamo!	**The Bonze, Yakusidé, Chorus** *(ST)* *[emphatically]* We renounced you!
Chorus *(ST)* Hou! Cio-cio-san! *[evening begins to close in]*	**Chorus** *(ST)* Hou! Cho-cho-san! *[evening begins to close in]*
Chorus *(S) [very far off]* Hou! Cio-cio-san! *[Butterfly burst into childish tears.* *Pinkerton hears her and anxiously* *hastens to her side, supporting her in her* *fainting condition and tenderly taking* *her hands from her tearful face]*	**Chorus** *(S) [very far off]* Hou!Cho-cho-san! *[Butterfly burst into childish tears.* *Pinkerton hears her and anxiously* *hastens to her side, supporting her in her* *fainting condition and tenderly taking* *her hands from her tearful face]*
Pinkerton Bimba, bimba, non piangere per gracchiar di ranocchi...	**Pinkerton** Darling, darling, don't cry let the frogs keep croaking…
Chorus *(S) [very far away]* Hou! Cio-cio-san!	**Chorus** *(S) [very far away]* Hou!Cho-cho-san!
Butterfly *[holding her ears, so as not to* *hear the shouts]* Urlano ancor!	**Butterfly** *[holding her ears, so as not to* *hear the shouts]* They're still yelling!
Pinkerton *[cheering her]* Tutta la tua tribù e i Bonzi tutti del Giappon non valgono il pianto di quegli occhi cari e belli.	**Pinkerton** *[cheering her]* All your tribes and the Bonzes in Japan are not worth a tear from eyes so sweet and gentle.

Italian	English
Butterfly [*smiling with childlike pleasure*] Davver? [*evening begins to fall*] Non piango più. E quasi del ripudio non mi duole per le vostre parole che mi suonan così dolci nel cor. [*stoops to kiss Pinkerton's hand*]	**Butterfly** [*smiling with childlike pleasure*] Really? [*evening begins to fall*] Then I'll cry no more. And I am not even worried for their repudiation with your words that sound so sweet in my heart. [*stoops to kiss Pinkerton's hand*]
Pinkerton [*gently stopping her*] Che fai?... la man?	**Pinkerton** [*gently stopping her*] What are you doing?... My hand?
Butterfly M'han detto che laggiù fra la gente costumata è questo il segno del maggior rispetto.	**Butterfly** They told me that abroad among the well-mannered people is a sign of the highest respect.
Suzuki [*within*] [*murmuring*] E Izaghi ed Izanami sarundasico, e Kami, e Izaghi ed Izanami sarundasico, e Kami.	**Suzuki** [*within*] [*murmuring*] And Izaghi and Izanami sarundasico, and Kami, and Izaghi and Izanami sarundasico, and Kami.
Pinkerton [*wondering at the subdued murmurs*] Chi brontola lassù?	**Pinkerton** [*wondering at the subdued murmurs*] Who's murmuring over there?
Butterfly È Suzuki che fa la sua preghiera seral. [*Evening draws in more and more and Pinkerton leads Butterfly towards the house*]	**Butterfly** It's Suzuki saying her evening prayer. [*Evening draws in more and more and Pinkerton leads Butterfly towards the house*]
Pinkerton Viene la sera	**Pinkerton** Evening is coming.

Italian	English
Butterfly e l'ombra e la quiete.	**Butterfly** with shadows and quiet.
Pinkerton E sei qui sola.	**Pinkerton** And you're here alone.
Butterfly Sola e rinnegata! Rinnegata... e felice!	**Butterfly** Alone and renounced! Renounced … And happy!
Pinkerton *[Pinkerton claps his hands thrice: the servants and Suzuki hasten in and Pinkerton orders:]* A voi, chiudete. *[the servants silently slide along several partitions]*	**Pinkerton** *[Pinkerton claps his hands thrice: the servants and Suzuki hasten in and Pinkerton orders:]* You, close all the doors. *[the servants silently slide along several partitions]*
Butterfly *[with deep feeling to Pinkerton]* Sì, sì, noi tutti soli... E fuori il mondo…	**Butterfly** *[with deep feeling to Pinkerton]* Yes, yes, we're all alone … And the world is out there…
Pinkerton *[laughing]* E il Bonzo furibondo. *[sits down and takes a cigarette]*	**Pinkerton** *[laughing]* And so is your furious uncle. *[sits down and takes a cigarette]*
Butterfly *[to Suzuki, who has come in with the servants is awaiting orders]* Suzuki, le mie vesti. *[Suzuki rummages in a trunk and gives Butterfly her night attire and a small box with toilet requirements.]*	**Butterfly** *[to Suzuki, who has come in with the servants is awaiting orders]* Suzuki, bring my robes. *[Suzuki rummages in a trunk and gives Butterfly her night attire and a small box with toilet requirements.]*
Suzuki *[bowing low to Pinkerton]* Buona notte. *[Pinkerton claps his hands, the servants run away].* *Butterfly retires to a corner at the back,*	**Suzuki** *[bowing low to Pinkerton]* Goodnight, sir. *[Pinkerton claps his hands, the servants run away].* *Butterfly retires to a corner at the back,*

Italian	English
and assisted by Suzuki, carefully performs her toilet for the night, exchanging her wedding-garment for one of pure white; then she sits down on a cushion and looking in a small hand-mirror arranges her hair. Suzuki goes out.	*and assisted by Suzuki, carefully performs her toilet for the night, exchanging her wedding-garment for one of pure white; then she sits down on a cushion and looking in a small hand-mirror arranges her hair. Suzuki goes out.*
Butterfly	**Butterfly**
Quest'obi pomposa	This huge obi
di scioglier mi tarda...	is delaying me…
si vesta la sposa	A bride must wear
di puro candor.	pure white robe.
Tra motti sommessi	Jokingly
sorride e mi guarda.	he smiles and looks at me.
Celarmi potessi!	I can't hide!
ne ho tanto rossor!	I'm blushing!
Pinkerton *[lounging on the wicker chair, watches Butterfly]*	**Pinkerton** *[lounging on the wicker chair, watches Butterfly]*
Con moti di scojattolo	Like a tender squirrel
i nodi allenta e scioglie!...	she slackens and loosens the knots!...
Pensar che quel giocattolo	To think that pretty dolly
è mia moglie. Mia moglie!	is my wife. My wife!
[smiling] Ma tal	*[smiling]* But such a charme
grazia dispiega,	is the reason why
ch'io	I am consumed
mi struggo per la febbre	with the fever
d'un subito desìo.	of this desire.
[rising, gradually draws closer to Butterfly]	*[rising, gradually draws closer to Butterfly]*
Butterfly	**Butterfly**
E ancor l'irata	I still hear the angry voices that
voce mi maledice...	curse me…
Butterfly rinnegata...	Butterfly renounced…
Rinnegata... e felice.	Renounced… Yet happy.

Italian	English
Pinkerton *[raises Butterfly gently, and goes out with her on the terrace]* Bimba dagli occhi pieni di malìa ora sei tutta mia. Sei tutta vestita di giglio. Mi piace la treccia tua bruna fra candidi veli.	**Pinkerton** *[raises Butterfly gently, and goes out with her on the terrace]* Child with the evil in your eyes now you're mine. You are robed all in pure lily whiteness. I like your brown braid among the white garments.
Butterfly *[goes down from the terrace, Pinkerton follows her]* Somiglio la Dea della luna, la piccola Dea della luna che scende la notte dal ponte del ciel.	**Butterfly** *[goes down from the terrace, Pinkerton follows her]* I am like the Moon Goddess, the little Moon Goddess who descends at night from her bridge in the sky.
Pinkerton E affascina i cuori...	**Pinkerton** And bewitches all hearts…
Butterfly E li prende, e li avvolge in un bianco mantel. E via se li reca negli alti reami,	**Butterfly** And she grabs them, and she wraps them in a white mantle And away she takes them to noble realms,
Pinkerton Ma intanto finor non m'hai detto, ancor non m'hai detto che m'ami. Le sa quella Dea le parole che appagan gli ardenti desir?	**Pinkerton** But meanwhile you haven't told me yet you haven't told me yet that you love me. Does that Goddess know the words that satisfy these burning desires
Butterfly Le sa. Forse dirle non vuole per tema d'averne a morir, per tema d'averne a morir!	**Butterfly** She does. Perhaps she doesn't want to say them fearing her death, fearing her death!
Pinkerton Stolta paura, l'amor non uccide	**Pinkerton** Stupid fear, love doesn't bring death

Italian	English
ma dà vita, e sorride per gioie celestiali *[drawing close to Butterfly and taking her face in his hands]* come ora fa nei tuoi lunghi occhi ovali. *[Butterfly, with a sudden movement, withdraws herself from Pinkerton's ardent embrace]*	but life, and it smiles of heavenly happiness *[drawing close to Butterfly and taking her face in his hands]* just as it now lights up your eyes. *[Butterfly, with a sudden movement, withdraws herself from Pinkerton's ardent embrace]*
Butterfly *[reticently]* Pensavo: se qualcuno mi volesse... *[stops short]*	**Butterfly** *[reticently]* I was thinking: if only someone wanted me… *[stops short]*
Pinkerton Perchè t'interrompi?	**Pinkerton** Why do you stutter?
Butterfly *[resuming, simply]* ...pensavo: se qualcuno mi volesse forse lo sposerei per qualche tempo. Fu allora che il nakodo le vostre nozze ci propose. Ma, vi dico in verità a tutta prima le propose invano. Un uomo americano! Un barbaro! una vespa! Scusate, non sapevo...	**Butterfly** *[resuming, simply]* … I was thinking: if only someone wanted me, perhaps for a time I'd have married. It was then that the Nakodo proposed to marry you. But, I must be sincere with you he made the same offer to all of us. A man from America! A foreigner! A stranger! Forgive me, I didn't know...
Pinkerton *[encouraging her to go on]* Amor mio dolce! E poi?.. Racconta...	**Pinkerton** *[encouraging her to go on]* My sweet love! And then?.. Go on…
Butterfly Adesso voi siete per me l'occhio del firmamento. E mi piaceste dal primo momento che vi ho veduto. *[Butterfly has a sudden panic and puts*	**Butterfly** Now you are to me the eye of the heavens. And I've loved you since the first time I saw you. *[Butterfly has a sudden panic and puts*

Italian	English
her hands to her ears, as though she still heard her relatives shouting; then she rallies and once more turns confidingly to Pinkerton.] Siete alto, forte. Ridete con modi si palesi! E dite cose che mai non intesi. Or son contenta, or son contenta. *[Night has closed in completely: the sky is unclouded and closely strewn with stars]*	*her hands to her ears, as though she still heard her relatives shouting; then she rallies and once more turns confidingly to Pinkerton.]* You are tall, strong. Your smile is so genuine! You tell me things that I never heard. Now I am happy, now I am happy. *[Night has closed in completely: the sky is unclouded and closely strewn with stars]*
Butterfly *[slowly drawing nearer to Pinkerton] [tenderly, almost beseechingly]* Vogliatemi bene, un bene piccolino, un bene da bambino quale a me si conviene, vogliatemi bene. Noi siamo gente avvezza alle piccole cose umili e silenziose, ad una tenerezza sfiorante e pur profonda come il ciel, come l'onda del mare.	**Butterfly** *[slowly drawing nearer to Pinkerton] [tenderly, almost beseechingly]* Love me, gently, just a very little, like a child that is all I can ask for, love me. We are people used to simple things humble and quiet, to a tender touch yet as profound as the sky, as the waves of the sea.
Pinkerton Dammi ch'io baci le tue mani care. *[bursts out very tenderly]* Mia Butterfly! come t'han ben nomata tenue farfalla... *[at these words Butterfly's face clouds over and she withdraws her hands]*	**Pinkerton** Let me kiss your darling hands. *[bursts out very tenderly]* My Butterfly! How suitably your name was chosen.... *[at these words Butterfly's face clouds over and she withdraws her hands]*

Italian	English
Butterfly Dicon ch'oltre mare se cade in man dell'uom, *[with an expression of fear]* ogni farfarla da uno spillo è trafitta *[with anguish]* ed in tavola infitta!..	**Butterfly** They say that overseas if a butterfly is caught by a man, *[with an expression of fear]* he'll pierce its heart with a pin. *[with anguish]* and exhibit it on a board!
Pinkerton *[taking her hands again gently, and smiling]* Un po' di vero c'è. E tu lo sai perchè? Perchè non fugga più. *[with ardour and embracing her affectionately]* Io t'ho ghermita... Ti serro palpitante. Sei mia.	**Pinkerton** *[taking her hands again gently, and smiling]* There's some truth in that. And do you know why? So she may not escape. *[with ardour and embracing her affectionately]* I have caught you… I hold you as you quake. You are mine.
Butterfly *[throwing herself into his arms]* Sì, per la vita.	**Butterfly** *[throwing herself into his arms]* Yes, for life.
Pinkerton Vieni, vieni... *[Butterfly draws back, as though ashamed of having been too bold]* Via dall'anima in pena l'angoscia paurosa. *[points to the starlit sky]* È notte serena! Guarda: dorme ogni cosa!	**Pinkerton** Come, come… *[Butterfly draws back, as though ashamed of having been too bold]* Free your lost soul from this fearful anguish. *[points to the starlit sky]* It's a quiet night! Look: all is sleeping!
Butterfly *[looking at the sky, enraptured]* Ah! Dolce notte!..	**Butterfly** *[looking at the sky, enraptured]* Ah! Sweet night!...

Italian	English
Pinkerton Vieni, vieni…	**Pinkerton** Come, come…
Butterfly Quante stelle! Non le vidi mai sì belle!	**Butterfly** So many stars! I've never seen them so beautiful!
Pinkerton È notte serena! Ah! vieni, vieni. È notte serena!.. Guarda: dorme ogni cosa!	**Pinkerton** It's a quiet night! Ah! Come, come. It's a quiet night!... Look: all is sleeping!
Butterfly Dolce notte! Quante stelle!	**Butterfly** Sweet night! So many stars!
Pinkerton Vieni, vieni!	**Pinkerton** Come, come!
Butterfly Non le vidi mai sì belle!	**Butterfly** I've never seen them so beautiful!
Pinkerton Vieni, vieni!	**Pinkerton** Come, come!
Butterfly Trema, brilla ogni favilla	**Butterfly** Trembling, sparkling each star in the sky
Pinkerton Vien, sei mia!...	**Pinkerton** Come, you are mine!...
Butterfly col baglior d'una pupilla. Oh! Oh! quanti occhi fisi, attenti d'ogni parte a riguardar! pei firmamenti, via pei lidi, via pel mare...	**Butterfly** Like a shining pupil. Oh! Oh! Like many eyes, careful the stars are gazing at us! through heavens, shores, across the sea…

Italian	English
Pinkerton [*with amorous desire*] Via l'angoscia dal tuo cor! Ti serro palpitante. Sei mia. Ah! Vien, vien sei mia ah! vieni, guarda: dorme ogni cosa!.. Ti serro palpitante. Ah, vien! **Butterfly** Ah! quanti occhi fisi, attenti! quanti sguardi! **Pinkerton** Guarda: dorme ogni cosa: Ah! vien! ah! vieni, vieni! Ah! vien, ah! vien, sei mia! ah! vien! **Butterfly** ride il ciel! Ah! Dolce notte! Tutto estatico d'amor ride il ciel! [*They go up from the garden into the house*]. *The curtain falls.*	**Pinkerton** [*with amorous desire*] Free yourself from the anguish in your heart! I hold you as you quake. You are mine. Ah! Come then, come you are mine ah! Come, look: all is sleeping!... I hold you as you quake. Ah, come! **Butterfly** Ah! So many shining stars! they're gazing at us! **Pinkerton** Look: all is sleeping: Ah! Come! Ah! Come, come then! Ah!Come, ah! Come, you are mine! Ah! come! **Butterfly** Sky is laughing! Ah! Sweet night! All ecstatic with love Sky is laughing! [*They go up from the garden into the house*]. *The curtain falls.*
End of Act I.	End of Act I.

Act II

Inside Butterfly's House

First Part

The curtain rises: - The curtains are drawn, leaving the room in semi-darkness. Suzuki, coiled up before the images of Buddha, is praying. From time to time she rings the prayer-bell. Butterfly is standing rigid and motionless near a screen.

Suzuki *[praying]*
E Izaghi ed Izanami,
Sarundasico e Kami...
[stopping short]
Oh! la mia testa!
[she rings the bell to invoke the attention of the Gods]
E tu
Ten-Sjoo-daj
[in tearful tones, looking at Butterfly]
fate che Butterfly
non pianga più, mai più, mai più!...

Butterfly *[without moving]*
Pigri ed obesi
son gli Dei Giapponesi!
L'americano Iddio son persuasa
ben più presto risponde a chi l'implori.

Ma temo ch'egli ignori
che noi stiam qui di casa.
[remains pensive]
Suzuki rises, draws back the curtains and slides back the partition at the back, towards the garden]

Suzuki *[praying]*
And Izaghi and Izanami,
Sarundasico and Kami…
[stopping short]
Oh! My head is spinning!
[she rings the bell to invoke the attention of the Gods]
And you
Ten-Sjoo-daj
[in tearful tones, looking at Butterfly]
Assure me that Butterfly
shall cry no more, no more, no more!...

Butterfly *[without moving]*
Lazy and fat
are the Japanese Gods!
I do believe that American God
provides a far more quickly response to prayers.
But I fear he doesn't know
we live here.
[remains pensive]
Suzuki rises, draws back the curtains and slides back the partition at the back, towards the garden]

Butterfly [turns to Suzuki]
Suzuki, è lungi la miseria?
[Suzuki goes to a small cabinet and
opens a casket to look for some money]

Suzuki [goes to Butterfly and shows her
a very few coins]
Questo
è l'ultimo fondo.

Butterfly
Questo? Oh! Troppe spese!
[Suzuki puts back the money into the
cabinet which she closes]

Suzuki [sighing]
S'egli non torna e presto,
siamo male in arnese.

Butterfly [with decision]
Ma torna.

Suzuki [shaking her head]
Tornerà!

Butterfly [vexed, approaches Suzuki]
Perché dispone
che il Console provveda alla pigione,
rispondi, su!
[Suzuki is silent]
[still persists]
Perché con tante cure
la casa rifornì di serrature,
s'ei non volessi ritornar mai più?

Suzuki
Non lo so.

Butterfly [turns to Suzuki]
Suzuki, how long before we're starving?
[Suzuki goes to a small cabinet and
opens a casket to look for some money]

Suzuki [goes to Butterfly and shows her
a very few coins]
This is
all we have left now.

Butterfly
No more? Oh! Too many expenses!
[Suzuki puts back the money into the
cabinet which she closes]

Suzuki [sighing]
Unless he returns and quickly,
we'll have many troubles.

Butterfly [with decision]
But he'll come back.

Suzuki [shaking her head]
He'll come!

Butterfly [vexed, approaches Suzuki]
Then why did he order the Consul
to pay for our rent,
now answer that!
[Suzuki is silent]
[still persists]
Why did he take so much care
to lock every entrance of the house
if he didn't intend to come back?

Suzuki
I don't know.

Butterfly [rather annoyed and surprised at such ignorance]
Non lo sai?
[calming down again and with proud confidence]
Io te lo dico. Per tener ben fuori
le zanzare, i parenti ed i dolori

e dentro, con gelosa
custodia, la sua sposa,
la sua sposa che son io, Butterfly.

Suzuki [still far from covinced]
Mai non s'è udito
di straniero marito
che sia tornato al suo nido.

Butterfly [furious, seizing hold of Suzuki]
Ah! Taci, o t'uccido.
[still trying to convince Suzuki]
Quell'ultima mattina:
tornerete signor? gli domandai.
Egli, col cuore grosso,
per celarmi la pena
sorridendo rispose:
``O Butterfly
piccina mogliettina,
tornerò colle rose
alla stagion serena
quando fa la nidiata il pettirosso."
[calm and convinced]
Tornerà.

Suzuki [incredulously]
Speriam:

Butterfly [insisting]
Dillo con me:

Butterfly [rather annoyed and surprised at such ignorance]
You don't know?
[calming down again and with proud confidence]
I'll tell you then. It was to keep away
those mosquitos, my relatives and their curses
and inside, to jealously
protect me, his beloved wife,
his bride who is me, Butterfly.

Suzuki [still far from covinced]
I've never heard
of a foreign husband
who came back to his nest.

Butterfly [furious, seizing hold of Suzuki]
Ah! Quiet, or I'll kill you.
[still trying to convince Suzuki]
That last morning:
Sir, will you come back? I asked him.
He, with his heavy heart,
to hide his pain
answered with a smile:
"Oh Butterfly
my sweet little child-wife,
I'll be back with the roses
during the shining season
when the robins are nesting"
[calm and convinced]
He will return.

Suzuki [incredulously]
Let's hope so:

Butterfly [insisting]
Say it with me:

Tornerà.	He will return.
Suzuki [to please her, she repeats, but mournfully]	**Suzuki** [to please her, she repeats, but mournfully]
Tornerà...	He will return…
[bursts into tears]	[bursts into tears]
Butterfly [surprised]	**Butterfly** [surprised]
Piangi? Perché? perché?	Are you crying? Why? Why?
Ah la fede ti manca!	Ah you are lacking faith!
[full of faith and smiling]	[full of faith and smiling]
Senti.	Listen to me.
[acts the scene as though it were actually taking place]	[acts the scene as though it were actually taking place]
Un bel dì, vedremo	One sunny day, we will see
levarsi un fil di fumo sull'estremo	a string of smoke n the far
confin del mare.	horizon.
E poi la nave appare.	and then a ship appears.
Poi la nave bianca	Then the white ship
entra nel porto, romba il suo saluto.	enters the harbour, and cannons roar a greeting.
Vedi? È venuto!	You see? He has come!
Io non gli scendo incontro. Io no. Mi metto	I do not go to greet him. Not I. I stand there
là sul ciglio del colle e aspetto, e aspetto	on the top of the hill just waiting,
gran tempo e non mi pesa,	waiting for a long time and I don't care,
la lunga attesa.	of the long waiting.
E... uscito dalla folla cittadina	And… from out of the crowded city
un uomo, un picciol punto	a man, a tiny speck
s'avvia per la collina.	makes his way up the hill.
Chi sarà? chi sarà?	Who can it be? Can you guess it?
E come sarà giunto	And when he's arrived
che dirà? che dirà?	What will he say? What will he say?
Chiamerà Butterfly dalla lontana.	He will call Butterfly from the distance.
Io senza dar risposta	I won't answer
me ne starò nascosta	I'll hide myself
un po' per celia e un po' per non morire	a bit to tease him and a bit so as not to
al primo incontro, ed egli alquanto in	die at our first meeting, then he'll be

pena
chiamerà, chiamerà:
Piccina mogliettina
olezzo di verbena,
i nomi che mi dava al suo venire.
[to Suzuki]
Tutto questo avverrà, te lo prometto.
Tienti la tua paura, io con sicura
fede l'aspetto.
[to Suzuki]out of the door on the left.
Butterfly looks after her sadly]
[Goro and Sharpless appear in the
garden: Goro looks into the room, sees
Butterfly through a window and says to
Sharpless who is following him:]

Goro
C'è. Entrate.
[Goro and Sharpless cross the garden]

Sharpless *[approaches and cautiously*
knocks at the door on the Right]
Chiedo scusa...
[Sharpless sees Butterfly, who hearing
someone come in, has risen.]
Madama Butterfly...

Butterfly *[corrects him without turning*
around]
Madama Pinkerton.
Prego.
[turns and recognizes the Consul, claps
her hands for joy]
Oh!
[Suzuki enters eagerly and prepares a
small table with smoking materials, some
cushions and a stool]
[joyfully]
il mio signor Console, signor Console!

worried
and will call, call:
My lovely wife
perfume of verbena,
the names he gave me when he was with
me. *[to Suzuki]*
These events will happen, I promise you.
Get rid of your fears, I await him with
strong faith.
[to Suzuki]out of the door on the left.
Butterfly looks after her sadly]
[Goro and Sharpless appear in the
garden: Goro looks into the room, sees
Butterfly through a window and says to
Sharpless who is following him:]

Goro
She's here. Come.
[Goro and Sharpless cross the garden]

Sharpless *[approaches and cautiously*
knocks at the door on the Right]
Forgive me…
[Sharpless sees Butterfly, who hearing
someone come in, has risen.]
Madam Butterfly...

Butterfly *[corrects him without turning*
around]
Madam Pinkerton.
Excuse me.
[turns and recognizes the Consul, claps
her hands for joy]
Oh!
[Suzuki enters eagerly and prepares a
small table with smoking materials,
some cushions and a stool]
[joyfully]
My dear Mr. Consul, mr. Consul!

Sharpless *[surprised]*
Mi ravvisate?

Butterfly *[doing the honours of the house]*
Ben venuto in casa
americana.

Sharpless
Grazie.
[Butterfly invites the Consul to sit near the table: Sharpless drops awkwardly onto a cushion: Butterfly sits down on the other side and smiles slyly behind her fan, on seeing the Consul's discomfort: then with great charm she asks him:]

Butterfly
Avi, antenati
tutti bene?

Sharpless *[thanks with a smile]*
Ma spero.

Butterfly *[signs to Suzuki to prepare the pipe]*
Fumate?

Sharpless
Grazie.
[anxious to explain the object of his visit, produces a letter from his pocket.]
Ho qui...

Butterfly *[interrupting him, without noticing the letter]*
Signore, io vedo
il cielo azzurro.

Sharpless *[surprised]*
Do you recognize me?

Butterfly *[doing the honours of the house]*
Welcome to
an American house.

Sharpless
Thank you.
[Butterfly invites the Consul to sit near the table: Sharpless drops awkwardly onto a cushion: Butterfly sits down on the other side and smiles slyly behind her fan, on seeing the Consul's discomfort: then with great charm she asks him:]

Butterfly
Are your
ancestors well?

Sharpless *[thanks with a smile]*
I hope so.

Butterfly *[signs to Suzuki to prepare the pipe]*
Do you smoke?

Sharpless
Thank you.
[anxious to explain the object of his visit, produces a letter from his pocket.]
I have here…

Butterfly *[interrupting him, without noticing the letter]*
Sir, I see a
cloudless sky.

[after having taken a draw at the pipe which Suzuki has prepared she offers it to the Consul]

Sharpless *[refusing]*
Grazie...
[again trying to resume the thread of his talk]
Ho...

Butterfly *[places the pipe on the table, and says very pressingly]*
Preferite
forse le sigarette
offers him one]
Americane?..

Sharpless *[rather annoyed, takes one]*
Ma grazie.
[tries to resume his talk]
Ho da mostrarvi...
[rises]

Butterfly *[hands Sharpless a lighted taper]*
A voi.

Sharpless *[lights the cigarette, but then puts it down at once and showing her the letter, sits on the stool]*
Mi scrisse
Mister Pinkerton...

Butterfly *[with intense eagerness]*
Davvero!
È in salute?

Sharpless
Perfetta.

[after having taken a draw at the pipe which Suzuki has prepared she offers it to the Consul]

Sharpless *[refusing]*
Thank you…
[again trying to resume the thread of his talk]
I have…

Butterfly *[places the pipe on the table, and says very pressingly]*
Do you prefer
maybe American
[offers him one]
cigarettes?..

Sharpless *[rather annoyed, takes one]*
Thank you.
[tries to resume his talk]
I have to show you..
[rises]

Butterfly *[hands Sharpless a lighted taper]*
For you.

Sharpless *[lights the cigarette, but then puts it down at once and showing her the letter, sits on the stool]*
I've a letter
from Mr. Pinkerton…

Butterfly *[with intense eagerness]*
Really?
Is he in good health?

Sharpless
He's well.

Butterfly *[jumping up very joyfully]*
Io son la donna
più lieta del Giappone.
[Suzuki is busy getting tea ready]
Potrei farvi
una domanda?

Sharpless
Certo.

Butterfly *[sits down again]*
Quando fanno
il lor nido in America
i pettirossi?

Sharpless *[amazed]*
Come dite?

Butterfly
Sì,...
prima o dopo di qui?

Sharpless
Ma... perchè?...
[Goro, who is sauntering round the garden, comes up on to the terrace and listens, unseen, to Butterfly]

Butterfly
Mio marito m'ha promesso
di ritornar nella stagion beata
che il pettirosso rifà la nidiata.
Qui l'ha rifatta per ben tre volte, ma
può darsi che di là
usi nidiar men spesso.
[Goro appears and bursts out laughing]
[turning round]
Chi ride?
[seeing Goro]

Butterfly *[jumping up very joyfully]*
I am the happiest
woman in Japan.
[Suzuki is busy getting tea ready]
Could I ask you
a question?

Sharpless
Surely.

Butterfly *[sits down again]*
When is the nesting time
in America
for robins?

Sharpless *[amazed]*
Are you serious?

Butterfly
Yes,...
earlier or later then here?

Sharpless
But… why this question?...
[Goro, who is sauntering round the garden, comes up on to the terrace and listens, unseen, to Butterfly]

Butterfly
My husband promised me
to return in the joyful season
when robins rebuild their nests.
Here they've nested three times already,
but perhaps I though over there robins
might nest less often.
[Goro appears and bursts out laughing]
[turning round]
Who's laughing?
[seeing Goro]

Oh, c'è il nakodo.
[seeing Goro]
Un uom cattivo.

Goro *[coming forward and bowing obsequiously]*
Godo...

Butterfly *[to Goro, who bows again and goes to help Suzuki]*
Zitto.
[to Sharpless]
Egli osò...
[changing her mind]
No, prima rispondete
alla dimanda mia.

Sharpless *[confused]*
Mi rincresce, ma ignoro...
Non ho studiato ornitologia,

Butterfly
orni...

Sharpless
...tologia.

Butterfly
Non lo sapete
insomma.

Sharpless
No.
[tries again to return to his point]
Dicevamo...

Butterfly *[interrupts him, following her thoughts]*
Ah, sì. Goro,

Oh, here's the nakodo.
[seeing Goro]
A scoundrel.

Goro *[coming forward and bowing obsequiously]*
I was...

Butterfly *[to Goro, who bows again and goes to help Suzuki]*
Quiet.
[to Sharpless]
He dared...
[changing her mind]
But first answer
my question.

Sharpless *[confused]*
I'm sorry, I don't know...
I haven't studied ornithology,

Butterfly
orni...

Sharpless
… thology.

Butterfly
Then
you don't know.

Sharpless
No.
[tries again to return to his point]
We were saying...

Butterfly *[interrupts him, following her thoughts]*
Ah, yes. Goro,

appena F. B. Pinkerton fu in mare
mi venne ad assediare
con ciarle e con presenti
per ridarmi ora questo, or quel marito.
Or promette tesori
per uno scimunito...

Goro *[intervenes, trying to justify himself and turning to Sharpless]*
Il ricco Yamadori.
Ella è povera in canna. I suoi parenti
l'han tutti rinnegata.
[Beyond the terrace the Prince Yamadori is seen, followed by two servants carrying flowers]

Butterfly *[sees Yamadori and points him out to Sharpless with a smile]*
Eccolo. Attenti.
Yamadori enters with great pomp from the door on the Right, followed by his two servants: Goro and Suzuki run up to him eagerly and go on their knees and hands before him. Then Suzuki takes the flowers and places them in various vases.
Yamadori greets the Consul, then bows most graciously to Butterfly. The two japanese servants having deposited the flowers, retire to the back, bowing deeply. Goro, servile and officious, places a stool for Yamadori between Sharpless and Butterfly, and is very much in evidence during the conversation. Butterfly, Sharpless and Yamadori sit down.

Butterfly
Yamadori ancor le pene

as soon as F.B. Pinkerton was away, bothered me
with arguments and proposals
to marry another man.
Or he promises treasures
from an idiot…

Goro *[intervenes, trying to justify himself and turning to Sharpless]*
The wealthy Yamadori.
She's very poor. Her relatives
have all renounced her.
[Beyond the terrace the Prince Yamadori is seen, followed by two servants carrying flowers]

Butterfly *[sees Yamadori and points him out to Sharpless with a smile]*
Here he is. Look.
Yamadori enters with great pomp from the door on the Right, followed by his two servants: Goro and Suzuki run up to him eagerly and go on their knees and hands before him. Then Suzuki takes the flowers and places them in various vases.
Yamadori greets the Consul, then bows most graciously to Butterfly. The two japanese servants having deposited the flowers, retire to the back, bowing deeply. Goro, servile and officious, places a stool for Yamadori between Sharpless and Butterfly, and is very much in evidence during the conversation. Butterfly, Sharpless and Yamadori sit down.

Butterfly
Yamadori, the pain of unrequited

dell'amor, non v'han deluso?
Vi tagliate ancor le vene
se il mio bacio vi ricuso?

Yamadori [to Sharpless]
Tra le cose più moleste
è l'inutil sospirar.

Butterfly [with graceful raillery]
Tante mogli omai toglieste,
vi doveste abituar.

Yamadori
L'ho sposate tutte quante
e il divorzio mi francò.

Butterfly
Obbligata.

Yamadori
A voi però
giurerei fede costante.

Sharpless [sighing, replaces the letter in his pocket]
(Il messaggio, ho gran paura,
a trasmetter non riesco.)

Goro [pointing out Yamadori to Sharpless, with emphasis]
Ville, servi, oro, ad Omara
un palazzo principesco.

Butterfly [seriously]
Già legata è la mia fede...

Goro and Yamadori [to Sharpless]
Maritata ancor si crede.

still hasn't disappointed you?
Do you still want to kill yourself
if I deny my kiss?

Yamadori [to Sharpless]
Among the most annoying things
is the pain of hopeless love.

Butterfly [with graceful raillery]
You've had many wives
that you should be used to that.

Yamadori
I've married all of them
and divorce has set me free.

Butterfly
Thank you kindly.

Yamadori
But yet to you
I would swear my faith forever.

Sharpless [sighing, replaces the letter in his pocket]
(I fear that my message,
will not be delivered.)

Goro [pointing out Yamadori to Sharpless, with emphasis]
Houses, servants, gold, at Omara
a regal palace.

Butterfly [seriously]
I am already married...

Goro and Yamadori [to Sharpless]
She still believes she's married.

Butterfly [rising from the cushion]
Non mi credo: sono, sono.

Goro
Ma la legge...

Butterfly
Io non la so.

Goro
...per la moglie, l'abbandono
al divorzio equiparò...

Butterfly
La legge giapponese...
non già del mio paese.

Goro
Quale?

Butterfly
Gli Stati Uniti.

Sharpless [to himself]
(Oh, l'infelice!)

Butterfly [strenuously, and growing excited]
Si sa che aprir la porta
e la moglie cacciar per la più corta
qui divorziar si dice.
Ma in America questo non si può.
[to Sharpless]
Vero?

Sharpless [embarrassed].
Vero... Però...

Butterfly [rising from the cushion]
I don't believe it: I am, I am.

Goro
But the law...

Butterfly
I don't know that law.

Goro
...for a wife, the abandon
it is equivalent to divorce...

Butterfly
Japanese law
it's not the law in my country.

Goro
Which country?

Butterfly
The United States.

Sharpless [to himself]
(Oh, poor sweet girl!)

Butterfly [strenuously, and growing excited]
It's known that here a man
shows his wife the doorway,
and it's effectively divorce.
But in America that cannot be done.
[to Sharpless]
That's so?

Sharpless [embarrassed].
True... But...

Butterfly [interrupts him, turning to Yamadori and Goro in triumph]
Là un bravo giudice
serio, impettito
dice al marito:
``Lei vuol andarsene?
Sentiam perché?"
``Sono seccato
del coniugato!"
E il magistrato:
[humourously]
``Ah, mascalzone,
presto in prigione!"
[to put an end to the subject, she orders Suzuki:]
Suzuki, il thè.
[Butterfly goes up to Suzuki who has already made the tea, and pours it into the cups.]

Yamadori [whispers to Sharpless]
Udiste?

Sharpless [whispers]
Mi rattrista una sì piena
cecità.

Goro [whispers to Sharpless and Yamadori]
Segnalata è già la nave
di Pinkerton.

Yamadori [in despair]
Quand'essa lo riveda...

Sharpless [whispers to both]
Egli non vuol mostrarsi. Io venni
appunto
per levarla d'inganno...

Butterfly [interrupts him, turning to Yamadori and Goro in triumph]
There a good judge
wise and impartial
says to the husband:
"You want to leave?
Let's hear why?"
"I'm sick and tired
of living together!"
And the judge:
[humourously]
"Ah, scoundrel,
lock him in prison!"
[to put an end to the subject, she orders Suzuki:]
Suzuki, tea!
[Butterfly goes up to Suzuki who has already made the tea, and pours it into the cups.]

Yamadori [whispers to Sharpless]
Did you hear that?

Sharpless [whispers]
I am grieved at
such blind ignorance.

Goro [whispers to Sharpless and Yamadori]
Pinkerton's ship
has been sighted.

Yamadori [in despair]
When she sees him again…

Sharpless [whispers to both]
He doesn't want to meet her. The reason
why I came here
was to explain it to her.

[seeing that Butterfly followed by Suzuki, is approaching him to offer him tea, cuts short his sentence]

Butterfly *[offering Sharpless tea]*
Vostra Grazia permette...
[opens her fan, and behind it points to the two others, laughing]
Che persone moleste!..
[then offers tea to Yamadori who refuses and rises to go]

Yamadori *[sighing]*
Addio. Vi lascio il cuor... pien di cordoglio:
ma spero ancor...

Butterfly
Padrone.

Yamadori *[Is going out, but returns into the room near Butterfly]*
Ah! se voleste...

Butterfly
Il guaio è che non voglio...
Yamadori, after having bowed to Sharpless, goes off sighing; he turns again with his hands on his heart, cutting a grotesque figure in the throes of love. The two servants follow him. Butterfly laughs again behind her fan and signs to Suzuki to remove the tea. Suzuki obeys, then retires to the back of the room.
Goro eagerly follows Yamadori.
Sharpless assumes a grave and serious aspect; with great respect, however, and some emotion, he invites Butterfly to be

[seeing that Butterfly followed by Suzuki, is approaching him to offer him tea, cuts short his sentence]

Butterfly *[offering Sharpless tea]*
Will Your Honor allow me...
[opens her fan, and behind it points to the two others, laughing]
What bothersome persons!...
[then offers tea to Yamadori who refuses and rises to go]

Yamadori *[sighing]*
Farewell. I leave you with my heart...
full of sorrow:
but I still have hope...

Butterfly
As you wish.

Yamadori *[Is going out, but returns into the room near Butterfly]*
Ah! If you would...

Butterfly
The pity is that I would not...
Yamadori, after having bowed to Sharpless, goes off sighing; he turns again with his hands on his heart, cutting a grotesque figure in the throes of love. The two servants follow him. Butterfly laughs again behind her fan and signs to Suzuki to remove the tea. Suzuki obeys, then retires to the back of the room.
Goro eagerly follows Yamadori.
Sharpless assumes a grave and serious aspect; with great respect, however, and some emotion, he invites Butterfly to be

seated, and once more draws the letter from his pocket

Sharpless
Ora a noi. Sedete qui,
[showing the letter]
legger con me volete
questa lettera?

Butterfly *[taking the letter]*
Date.
[kissing it] Sulla bocca,
[placing it on her heart] sul cuore...
[to Sharpless, prettily]
Siete l'uomo migliore
del mondo.
[gives back the letter and settles herself to listen with the greatest attention]
Incominciate.

Sharpless *[reading]*
``Amico, cercherai
quel bel fior di fanciulla."

Butterfly *[can no longer contain herself and exclaims joyfully]*
Dice proprio così?

Sharpless *[gravely]*
Sì, così dice,
ma se ad ogni momento...

Butterfly *[calming down again to listen]*
Taccio, taccio, più nulla.

Sharpless
``Da quel tempo felice,
tre anni son passati"

---

seated, and once more draws the letter from his pocket

Sharpless
Now, sit here,
[showing the letter]
would you like to read with me
this letter?

Butterfly *[taking the letter]*
Show me.
[kissing it] On my lips,
[placing it on her heart] on my heart...
[to Sharpless, prettily]
You are the best man
in this world.
[gives back the letter and settles herself to listen with the greatest attention]
Begin.

Sharpless *[reading]*
"My friend, you will look up
that sweet flower."

Butterfly *[can no longer contain herself and exclaims joyfully]*
Did he really say that?

Sharpless *[gravely]*
Yes, he did,
but if you interrupt at every moment...

Butterfly *[calming down again to listen]*
I'll be quiet.

Sharpless
"Since those joyful days,
three years have passed"

Butterfly [interrupting the reading]
Anche lui li ha contati!...

Sharpless [resumes]
``E forse Butterfly
non mi rammenta più."

Butterfly [very surprised, turning to Suzuki]
Non lo rammento?
Suzuki, dillo tu.
[repeats as though scandalized at the words of the letter]
``Non mi rammenta più!"
[Suzuki goes out through the door on the left]

Sharpless [to himself]
(Pazienza!)
[continues reading]
``Se mi vuol
bene ancor, se m'aspetta"

Butterfly [taking the letter from Sharpless' hands exclaims very tenderly]
Oh le dolci parole!
[kissing the letter]
Tu, benedetta!

Sharpless [takes the letter back and boldly resumes reading though his voice is trembling with emotion]
``A voi mi raccomando
perchè vogliate con circospezione
prepararla...

Butterfly [anxious, but joyful]
Ritorna…

Butterfly [interrupting the reading]
Then he too has been counting!...

Sharpless [resumes]
"And perhaps Butterfly doesn't
remember me anymore."

Butterfly [very surprised, turning to Suzuki]
I don't remember him?
Suzuki, tell him.
[repeats as though scandalized at the words of the letter]
"She doesn't remember me anymore!"
[Suzuki goes out through the door on the left]

Sharpless [to himself]
(Patience!)
[continues reading]
"If she still
loves me, if she's still waiting for me"

Butterfly [taking the letter from Sharpless' hands exclaims very tenderly]
Oh what sweet words!
[kissing the letter]
You, blessed letter!

Sharpless [takes the letter back and boldly resumes reading though his voice is trembling with emotion]
"On you I am relying
to act discreetly to
prepare her…

Butterfly [anxious, but joyful]
He's returning…

Sharpless
al colpo..."

Butterfly *[rises, jumping for joy and clapping her hands]*
Quando?
Presto! presto!

Sharpless *[taking a deep breath]*
(Benone).
[puts the letter away again]
[to himself] (Qui troncarla conviene...
[angrily] Quel diavolo d'un Pinkerton!)
[rises, then looks straight into Butterfly's eyes, very gravely]
Ebbene,
che fareste, Madama Butterfly...
s'ei non dovesse ritornar più mai?
[Butterfly, motionless as tho' she had received a death-blow, bows her head and replies with childlike submissiveness, almost stammering]

Butterfly
Due cose potrei far:
tornar... a divertir
la gente col cantar...
oppur,... meglio, morire.
[Sharpless is deeply moved and walks up and down excitedly; then he turns to Butterfly, takes her hands in his and says to her with fatherly tenderness]

Sharpless
Di strapparvi assai mi costa
dai miraggi ingannatori.
Accogliete la proposta
di quel ricco Yamadori.

Sharpless
for the shock..."

Butterfly *[rises, jumping for joy and clapping her hands]*
When?
Quickly! Quickly!

Sharpless *[taking a deep breath]*
(Enough).
[puts the letter away again]
[to himself] (It's best to stop here...
[angrily] That demon of Pinkerton!)
[rises, then looks straight into Butterfly's eyes, very gravely]
Well,
what would you do, Madam Butterfly...
If he should not return?
[Butterfly, motionless as tho' she had received a death-blow, bows her head and replies with childlike submissiveness, almost stammering]

Butterfly
Just two things I might do:
return... to amuse
people with my songs...
or, ... even better, die.
[Sharpless is deeply moved and walks up and down excitedly; then he turns to Butterfly, takes her hands in his and says to her with fatherly tenderness]

Sharpless
It's hard for me to tear you from
your sweet illusion.
Accept wealthy Yamadori's
proposal.

Butterfly *[in a voice broken by weeping, and withdrawing her hands]*
Voi, voi, signor, mi dite questo!... Voi?

Sharpless *[embarrased]*
Santo Dio, come si fa?

Butterfly *[claps her hands and Suzuki hastens in]*
Qui, Suzuki, presto presto,
che Sua Grazia se ne va.

Sharpless *[is on the point of going out]*
Mi scacciate?
[Butterfly, repenting, runs to Sharpless sobbing and holds him back]

Butterfly
Ve ne prego,
già l'insistere non vale.
[dismisses Suzuki who goes into the garden]

Sharpless *[making excuses]*
Fui brutale, non lo nego.

Butterfly *[mournfully, laying her hand on her heart]*
Oh, mi fate tanto male,
tanto male, tanto, tanto!
[Butterfly totters, Sharpless is about to support her, but she rallies quickly]

Butterfly
Niente, niente!...
Ho creduto morir... Ma passa presto
come passan le nuvole sul mare...
[making up her mind]
Ah! m'ha scordata?

Butterfly *[in a voice broken by weeping, and withdrawing her hands]*
You, you, sir. You tell me this!... You?

Sharpless *[embarrased]*
Oh dear God, what can I do?

Butterfly *[claps her hands and Suzuki hastens in]*
Come here, Suzuki, quickly, quickly,
Your Honor is leaving.

Sharpless *[is on the point of going out]*
You dismiss me?
[Butterfly, repenting, runs to Sharpless sobbing and holds him back]

Butterfly
Please,
keep insisting is useless.
[dismisses Suzuki who goes into the garden]

Sharpless *[making excuses]*
I was rude, I don't deny it.

Butterfly *[mournfully, laying her hand on her heart]*
Oh, you have hurt me
so deeply, so, so deeply!
[Butterfly totters, Sharpless is about to support her, but she rallies quickly]

Butterfly
It's nothing, nothing!...
I thought I was about to die... But it has
passed like the clouds across the sea...
[making up her mind]
Ah! Has he forgotten me?

[Butterfly runs into the room on the left]
[Butterfly returns triumphantly carrying her baby on her left shoulder, and shows him to Sharpless full of pride]

Butterfly
E questo?... e questo?... e questo
egli potrà pure scordare?..
[puts the child down on the ground and holds him close to her]

Sharpless *[with emotion]*
Egli è suo?

Butterfly *[pointing to each feature]*
Chi vide mai
a bimbo del Giappon occhi azzurrini?
E il labbro? E i ricciolini
d'oro schietto?

Sharpless *[more and more moved]*
È palese.
E Pinkerton lo sa?

Butterfly
No. No.
[passionately]
È nato quand'egli sta va
in quel suo gran paese.
Ma voi...
[caressing the child]
gli scriverete che l'aspetta
un figlio senza pari!
e mi saprete dir s'ei non s'affretta
per le terre e pei mari!
[putting the baby down on the cushion]
[kisses the child tenderly]
Sai cos'ebbe cuore
di pensare quel signore?

[Butterfly runs into the room on the left]
[Butterfly returns triumphantly carrying her baby on her left shoulder, and shows him to Sharpless full of pride]

Butterfly
And this?... And this?... and this
Can he forget this?
[puts the child down on the ground and holds him close to her]

Sharpless *[with emotion]*
He is his baby?

Butterfly *[pointing to each feature]*
Who ever saw
a Japanese child with blue eyes?
And his lips? And his head
with golden curls?

Sharpless *[more and more moved]*
It's obvious.
Does Pinkerton know it?

Butterfly
No. No.
[passionately]
The child was born when he was away
in his great country.
But you...
[caressing the child]
will write him that a son without equal
is waiting for his father!
then he will hasten
over land and over sea!
[putting the baby down on the cushion]
[kisses the child tenderly]
Do you know what that
gentleman was thinking in his heart?

[pointing to Sharpless]
Che tua madre dovrà
prenderti in braccio ed alla pioggia e al vento
andar per la città
a guadagnarti il pane e il vestimento.
Ed alle impietosite
genti, ballando de' suoi canti al suon,
gridare: ``Udite, udite
la bellissima canzon
delle ottocentomila
divinità vestite di splendor.''
E passerà una fila
di guerrieri coll' Imperator,
[holding up the child and fondling it]
cui dirò: ``Sommo Duce
ferma i tuoi servi e sosta a riguardar
quest'occhi, ove la luce
dal cielo azzurro onde scendesti appar.
[crouches down by the child and continues in caressing and tearful tones]
E allor fermato il piè
l'Imperatore d'ogni grazia degno,
forse, forse farà di te
il principe più bello del suo regno.
[laying her cheek next to the baby's cheek]
[She strains the child to her heart, then crouching down on the ground hugs him passionately.]

Sharpless *[cannot restrain his tears]*
(Quanta pietà!)
[conquering his emotion]
Vien sera. Io scendo al piano.
Mi perdonate?..
[Butterfly rises to her feet and with a charming gesture gives Sharpless her

[pointing to Sharpless]
That your mother should take you
in her arms and that should wander in the storm
through the city streets
begging for food and clothes.
And to the pitying people,
dancing at her singing, cry out:
"Listen, listen to this
lovely song
of all eight hundred thousand
magnificently dressed Gods."
Then a row of warriors
will pass with the Emperor,
[holding up the child and fondling it]
and I'll say to him: " Divine Ruler
please stop your servants and stare at
these blue eyes, blue as the heaven
you descends from.
[crouches down by the child and continues in caressing and tearful tones]
And when the Emperor, full of gracious
goodness, will stop his march
then perhaps he'll make you
the beautiful prince in his kingdom.
laying her cheek next to the baby's cheek]
[She strains the child to her heart, then crouching down on the ground hugs him passionately.]

Sharpless *[cannot restrain his tears]*
(So pitiful!)
[conquering his emotion]
It's evening. I must be going.
Will you forgive me?..
[Butterfly rises to her feet and with a charming gesture gives Sharpless her

hand; he shakes it cordially with both of his]

Butterfly [turning to the child]
A te, dagli la mano:

Sharpless [taking the child in his arms]
I bei capelli biondi!
[kisses it *]
Caro: come ti chiamano?

Butterfly [to the baby, with childlike grace]
Rispondi:
Oggi il mio nome è *Dolore*. Però
dite al babbo, scrivendogli, che il giorno
del suo ritorno,
Gioia, Gioia mi chiamerò.

Sharpless
Tuo padre lo saprà, te lo prometto...
[puts down the child, bows to Butterfly
and goes out quickly by door on the
right]

Suzuki [from outside, shouting]
Vespa! Rospo maledetto!
[Suzuki enters dragging in Goro
roughly, who tries to escape]
[loud cries from Goro *]

Butterfly [to Suzuki]
Che fu?

Suzuki
Ci ronza intorno
il vampiro! e ogni giorno
ai quattro venti
spargendo va

hand; he shakes it cordially with both of his]

Butterfly [turning to the child]
Now give me your hand:

Sharpless [taking the child in his arms]
What pretty golden hair!
[kisses it *]
Darling: what is your name?

Butterfly [to the baby, with childlike grace]
Answer him:
Today my name is *Sorrow*. But when
you write my father, tell him that when
he'll return
my name will be *Joy, Joy*.

Sharpless
Your father will know it, I promise you...
[puts down the child, bows to Butterfly
and goes out quickly by door on the
right]

Suzuki [from outside, shouting]
Wasp! Deplorable toad!
[Suzuki enters dragging in Goro
roughly, who tries to escape]
[loud cries from Goro *]

Butterfly [to Suzuki]
Who's that?

Suzuki
He buzzes around
like a vampire! and everyday
around the city spreads the story
that no one

che niuno sa
chi padre al bimbo sia!
[releases Goro]

Goro *[protesting in frightened tones]*
Dicevo... solo...
che là in America
[approaching the child and pointing to him]
quando un figliolo
è nato maledetto
[Butterfly instinctively stands in front of the child as though to protect him]
trarrà sempre reietto
la vita fra le genti!

Butterfly *[wild cry]*
[runs to the shrine and takes down the dagger which is hanging up]

Butterfly *[in wild tones]*
Ah! tu menti! menti! menti!
Ah! menti!
[Butterfly seizes Goro, who falls down, and threatens to kill him. Goro utters loud, desperate and prolonged howls.]
Dillo ancora e t'uccido!

Suzuki *[thrusts herself between them; then horrified at such a scene, she takes the child and carries him into the room on the left]*
No!

Butterfly *[seized with disgust she pushes him away with her foot]*
Va via!
[Goro makes his escape.]
[Butterfly remains motionless as though

knows who
the child's father is!
[releases Goro]

Goro *[protesting in frightened tones]*
I only… said…
that in America
[approaching the child and pointing to him]
when a child
is born in such shame
[Butterfly instinctively stands in front of the child as though to protect him]
he will be rejected
and avoided by people!

Butterfly *[wild cry]*
[runs to the shrine and takes down the dagger which is hanging up]

Butterfly *[in wild tones]*
Ah! You're lying! You're lying!
Ah! You're lying!
[Butterfly seizes Goro, who falls down, and threatens to kill him. Goro utters loud, desperate and prolonged howls.]
Say it again and I'll kill you!

Suzuki *[thrusts herself between them; then horrified at such a scene, she takes the child and carries him into the room on the left]*
No!

Butterfly *[seized with disgust she pushes him away with her foot]*
Get going!
[Goro makes his escape.]
[Butterfly remains motionless as though

petrified.]
[By degrees she rouses herself and goes to put away the dagger.]

Butterfly *[letting her thoughts fly to her child]*
Vedrai, piccolo amor,
mia pena e mio conforto,
mio piccolo amor,
Ah! vedrai
che il tuo vendicator
ci porterà lontano, lontan, nella sua terra,
lontan ci porterà.
[a cannon shot]*

Suzuki *[coming in breathlessly]*
Il cannone del porto!
Una nave da guerra...
[Butterfly and Suzuki run towards the terrace.]

Butterfly
Bianca... bianca... il vessillo americano
delle stelle... Or governa
per ancorare.
[takes a telescope from the table and runs on to the terrace to look out]
[all trembling with excitement, directs the telescope towards the harbour, and says to Suzuki]
Reggimi la mano
ch'io ne discerna
il nome, il nome, il nome. Eccolo:
ABRAMO LINCOLN!
[gives the telescope to Suzuki, and goes down from the terrace in the greatest state of excitement]
Tutti han mentito!
tutti!.. tutti!.. sol io

petrified.]
[By degrees she rouses herself and goes to put away the dagger.]

Butterfly *[letting her thoughts fly to her child]*
You see, my lovely boy,
my pain and my comfort,
my little love,
Ah! You will see
that your avenger
will take us far, far away to his country,
he will take us afar.
[a cannon shot]*

Suzuki *[coming in breathlessly]*
The cannon of the harbor!
A warship…
[Butterfly and Suzuki run towards the terrace.]

Butterfly
It's white… white… with the
American flag… It's entering the harbor
to anchor.
[takes a telescope from the table and runs on to the terrace to look out]
[all trembling with excitement, directs the telescope towards the harbour, and says to Suzuki]
Hold my hand
so I can ready the
name, the name, the name. Here it is:
ABRAHAM LINCOLN!
[gives the telescope to Suzuki, and goes down from the terrace in the greatest state of excitement]
They all lied!
Liars!... All of them!... Only I

lo sapevo sol io che l'amo.
[to Suzuki]
Vedi lo scimunito
tuo dubbio? È giunto! è giunto! è giunto!

proprio nel punto
che ognun diceva; piangi e dispera.
Trionfa il mio amor!
il mio amor;
la mia fè trionfa intera.
Ei torna e m'ama!
[rejoicing, runs on to the terrace]
[to Suzuki who has followed her unto the terrace]
Scuoti quella fronda
di ciliegio
e m'innonda di fior.
Io vo' tuffar nella pioggia odorosa
[sobbing with tenderness]
l'arsa fronte.

Suzuki [soothing her]
Signora,
quetatevi... quel pianto -

Butterfly [returns to the room with Suzuki]
No: rido, rido! Quanto
lo dovremo aspettar?
Che pensi? Un'ora?

Suzuki
Di più.

Butterfly
Due ore forse.
[walking up and down the room]
Tutto tutto sia pien
di fior, come la notte è di faville.

---

knew it, only I who love him.
[to Suzuki]
Now do you see the absurdity
of doubting? He's come!He's come!He's come!

right at the moment when
you were all saying; cry and suffer.
My love has won!
my love;
and my faith have won completely.
He's coming and still loves me!
[rejoicing, runs on to the terrace]
[to Suzuki who has followed her unto the terrace]
Shake that
cherry tree branch
so every flower can flutter down
and I want to plunge in a sweet scented
rain [sobbing with tenderness]
my burning brow.

Suzuki [soothing her]
Madame,
do calm yourself... that crying-

Butterfly [returns to the room with Suzuki]
No: I'm laughing! When
may we expect him?
What do you think? An hour?

Suzuki
More.

Butterfly
Two hours, more likely.
[walking up and down the room]
Flowers must fill this house,
just like the stars that fill the heavens.

[signs to Suzuki to go into the garden]
[to Suzuki]
Va pei fior.

Suzuki *[from the terrace]*
Tutti i fior?...

Butterfly *[gaily to Suzuki]*
Tutti i fior, tutti...
tutti. Pesco, vïola, gelsomin,
quanto di cespo, o d'erba, o d'albero fiorì.

Suzuki *[still on the terrace]*
Uno squallor d'inverno sarà tutto il
giardin.
[goes down into the garden]

Butterfly
Tutta la primavera voglio che olezzi qui.

Suzuki *[from the garden]*
Uno squallor d'inverno sarà tutto il
giardin.
*[appears on the terrace with a bunch of
flowers which she holds out to Butterfly]*
A voi signora.

Butterfly *[taking the flowers from
Suzuki's hands]*
Cogline ancora.
*[Butterfly distributes the flowers about
the room, while Suzuki goes down into
the garden again]*

Suzuki *[from the garden]*
Soventi a questa siepe veniste a
riguardare

[signs to Suzuki to go into the garden]
[to Suzuki]
Fetch the flowers.

Suzuki *[from the terrace]*
Every flower?...

Butterfly *[gaily to Suzuki]*
Pick them all…
All. Peaches, violets, jasmine,
just pick anything that has bloomed on
bush, grass or tree.

Suzuki *[still on the terrace]*
The garden will appear bare like winter.

[goes down into the garden]

Butterfly
I want the sweet scent of springtime to
fill the air.

Suzuki *[from the garden]*
The garden will appear bare like winter.

*[appears on the terrace with a bunch of
flowers which she holds out to Butterfly]*
A voi signora.

Butterfly *[taking the flowers from
Suzuki's hands]*
Pick some more.
*[Butterfly distributes the flowers about
the room, while Suzuki goes down into
the garden again]*

Suzuki *[from the garden]*
How often at this hedge you stood
gazing

lungi, piangendo nella deserta
immensità.

Butterfly
Giunse l'atteso, nulla più chiedo al mare;

diedi pianto alla zolla, essa i suoi fior mi
dà.

Suzuki [reappears on the terrace, laden
with flowers]
Spoglio è l'orto.

Butterfly
Spoglio è l'orto?
Vien, m'aiuta.

Suzuki
Rose al varco
della soglia.
[They scatter flowers everywhere]

Butterfly
Tutta la primavera

Suzuki
Tutta la primavera

Butterfly
voglio che olezzi qui.

Suzuki
voglio che olezzi qui.

Butterfly
Seminiamo intorno april,

Suzuki
Seminiamo intorno april.

across the ocean and
weeping at all that emptiness.

Butterfly
The man I awaited has returned, I no
longer pray the sea;
my crying watered the earth with tears
and now there are flowers.

Suzuki [reappears on the terrace, laden
with flowers]
There are no flowers.

Butterfly
There are no flowers?
Come and help me.

Suzuki
Roses shall deck
the threshold.
[They scatter flowers everywhere]

Butterfly
Let every scent of springtime

Suzuki
Let every scent of springtime

Butterfly
perfume the air with joy.

Suzuki
perfume the air with joy.

Butterfly
Let us make it April here,

Suzuki
Let us make it April here.

Butterfly
seminiamo april.

Butterfly [scattering flowers]
Tutta la primavera
voglio che olezzi qui...

Suzuki
Tutta la primavera, tutta, tutta.
Gigli?.. viole?..

Butterfly
intorno, intorno spandi.

Suzuki
Seminiamo intorno april.

Butterfly
Seminiamo intorno april.
Il suo sedil s'inghirlandi,
di convolvi s'inghirlandi;
gigli e viole intorno spandi,
seminiamo intorno april!

Suzuki
Gigli, rose spandi,
tutta la primavera,
spandi gigli, viole,
seminiamo intorno april!

Butterfly, Suzuki [scattering flowers
while they sway their bodies lightly to
and fro to the rhythm in a dance
measure]
Gettiamo a mani piene
mammole e tuberose,
corolle di verbene,
petali d'ogni fior!
corolle di verbene,

Butterfly
Let us make it April here,

Butterfly [scattering flowers]
Let every scent of springtime
perfume the air with joy…

Suzuki
Every scent of springtime
Lilies?..Violets?...

Butterfly
Spread them all around.

Suzuki
Let us make it April here.

Butterfly
Let us make it April here.
Let's deck his chair
with a garland,
Lilies and violets let us spread,
Let us make it April here!

Suzuki
Lilies, roses spread,
every scent of springtime,
let us spread lilies and violets,
we will make it April here!

Butterfly, Suzuki [scattering flowers
while they sway their bodies lightly to
and fro to the rhythm in a dance
measure]
In handfuls let us spread
violets and tuberoses,
corollas of verbenas,
petals of every flower!
corollas of verbenas,

petali d'ogni fior!
[Butterfly and Suzuki bring toilet requirements]

Butterfly *[to Suzuki]*
Or vienmi ad adornar.
[The sun begins to set] No! pria portami il bimbo.
[Suzuki goes into the room on the left, and fetches out the baby whom she seats next to Butterfly; while the latter looks at herself in a small hand-mirror and says sadly]
Non son più quella!...
Troppi sospiri la bocca mandò,...
e l'occhio riguardò
nel lontan troppo fiso.
[throws herself on the ground, laying her head on Suzuki's feet] [ardently]
Suzuki, fammi bella, fammi bella,
[raises her head and looks into Suzuki's face, crying bitterly]
fammi bella!

Suzuki *[caresing Butterfly's head to sooth her]*
Gioia, riposo accrescono beltà.

Butterfly *[pensively]*
Chissà! chissà!
[rising, goes back to her toilet]
chissà! chissà!
[to Suzuki]
Dammi sul viso
un tocco di carmino...
[takes a paint brush and puts a dab of rouge on the baby's cheeks]
ed anche a te piccino

petals of every flower!
[Butterfly and Suzuki bring toilet requirements]

Butterfly *[to Suzuki]*
Now I need to look my best.
[The sun begins to set] No! First bring me the baby.
[Suzuki goes into the room on the left, and fetches out the baby whom she seats next to Butterfly; while the latter looks at herself in a small hand-mirror and says sadly]
How much I've changed!...
So much sighing has marked my face,...
and my eyes stared too long at the ocean
and now they're tired.
[throws herself on the ground, laying her head on Suzuki's feet] [ardently]
Suzuki, makes me pretty, makes me pretty, *[raises her head and looks into Suzuki's face, crying bitterly]*
makes me pretty!

Suzuki *[caresing Butterfly's head to sooth her]*
Joy and rest make you prettier.

Butterfly *[pensively]*
Who knows! Who knows!
[rising, goes back to her toilet]
Who knows! Who knows!
[to Suzuki]
Put on my cheeks
a little touch of carmine...
[takes a paint brush and puts a dab of rouge on the baby's cheeks]
And also on you, my darling

perché la veglia non ti faccia vôte
per pallore le gote.

Suzuki *[urging her to keep quiet]*
Non vi movete che v'ho a ravviare i
capelli.

Butterfly *[following up an idea she has had]*
Che ne diranno!..
E lo zio Bonzo?..
[with a touch of fury]
già del mio danno
tutti contenti!..
[smiling]
E Yamadori
coi suoi languori!
Beffati,
scornati,
beffati,
spennati
gli ingrati!

Suzuki *[has finished her toilet]*
È fatto.

Butterfly *[to Suzuki]*
L'obi che vestii da sposa.
Qua ch'io lo vesta.
*[while Butterfly dons her garment,
Suzuki dresses the baby in the other one,
wrapping him up almost entirely in the
ample and light draperies]*
Vo' che mi veda indosso
il vel del primo dì.
*[to Suzuki, who has finished dressing the
baby]*
E un papavero rosso
nei capelli...

so that our waiting may not make your
face pale.

Suzuki *[urging her to keep quiet]*
Don't move until I've set your
hair.

Butterfly *[following up an idea she has had]*
What will they say!
And uncle Bonze?...
[with a touch of fury]
They were all pleased
with my disgrace!...
[smiling]
And Yamadori
and his languors!
Despised,
Scorned,
despised
Fleeced
those ingrates!

Suzuki *[has finished her toilet]*
It is finished.

Butterfly *[to Suzuki]*
The obi I wore at my wedding.
I want to wear it now.
*[while Butterfly dons her garment,
Suzuki dresses the baby in the other one,
wrapping him up almost entirely in the
ample and light draperies]*
I want him to see me like on our
wedding day.
*[to Suzuki, who has finished dressing the
baby]*
A red poppy
in my hair…

[Suzuki places the flower in Butterfly's hair. The latter is pleased with the effect]

Così.
[with childlike grace she signs to Suzuki to close the shosi*]*
Nello *shosi* farem tre forellini
per riguardar,
e starem zitti come topolini
ad aspettar.
[Suzuki closes the shosi *at the back]*
[the night grows darker]
[Butterfly leads the baby to the shosi*]*
Butterfly makes three holes in the shosi:
one high up for herself, one lower down for Suzuki and a third lower still for the child whom she seats on a cushion, signing to him to look through his hole. Suzuki crouches down and also gazes out. Butterfly stands in front of the highest hole and gazes through it, remaining rigid and motionless as a statue: the baby, who is between his mother and Suzuki, peeps out curiously. [It is night, the rays of the moon light up the shosi *from without]*

Chorus *(ST) [within, from far off]*
[humming]

[The baby falls asleep, sinking down on his cushion; Suzuki still in her crouching position, falls asleep too: Butterfly alone remains rigid and motionless].
[The curtain falls slowly]

End of Act II First Part.

[Suzuki places the flower in Butterfly's hair. The latter is pleased with the effect]

Like this.
[with childlike grace she signs to Suzuki to close the shosi*]*
We'll make three little holes here in the shoji so we can look,
we'll be as quiet as little mice waiting.
[Suzuki closes the shosi *at the back]*
[the night grows darker]
[Butterfly leads the baby to the shosi*]*
Butterfly makes three holes in the shosi:
one high up for herself, one lower down for Suzuki and a third lower still for the child whom she seats on a cushion, signing to him to look through his hole. Suzuki crouches down and also gazes out. Butterfly stands in front of the highest hole and gazes through it, remaining rigid and motionless as a statue: the baby, who is between his mother and Suzuki, peeps out curiously. [It is night, the rays of the moon light up the shosi *from without]*

Chorus *(ST) [within, from far off]*
[humming]

[The baby falls asleep, sinking down on his cushion; Suzuki still in her crouching position, falls asleep too: Butterfly alone remains rigid and motionless].
[The curtain falls slowly]

End of Act II First Part.

Act II

Second Part

Sailors *(T1) [from the bay, far away in the distance]* Oh eh! oh eh! **Sailors** *(T2)* Oh eh! **Sailors** *(T1)* oh eh! oh eh! **Sailors** *(T2)* oh eh! **Sailors** *(T1)* oh eh! oh eh! **Sailors** *(T2)* oh eh! **Sailors** *(T1)* Oh eh! oh eh! **Sailors** *(T2)* oh eh! **Sailors** *(T1)* oh eh! oh eh! **Sailors** *(T2)* oh eh! *[Clanging of chains, anchors, and other*	**Sailors** *(T1) [from the bay, far away in the distance]* Oh eh! oh eh! **Sailors** *(T2)* Oh eh! **Sailors** *(T1)* oh eh! oh eh! **Sailors** *(T2)* oh eh! **Sailors** *(T1)* oh eh! oh eh! **Sailors** *(T2)* oh eh! **Sailors** *(T1)* Oh eh! oh eh! **Sailors** *(T2)* oh eh! **Sailors** *(T1)* oh eh! oh eh! **Sailors** *(T2)* oh eh! *[Clanging of chains, anchors, and other*

sounds from the harbour]
[The curtain rises]
*[Butterfly, still motionless, is gazing
out into the distance; the child the child is
asleep on a cushion; and Suzuki,
kneeling bent over the child, has also
fallen asleep]*
*[The first streaks of dawn appear in the
sky]*
[The rosy dawn spreads]
[The day breaks].
[The sunshine streams in from outside]
*[Butterfly at length rouses herself, and
touches Suzuki on the shoulder; the
latter
wakes with a start and rises, whilst
Butterfly turns toward the baby, and
takes him up with tender care]*

Suzuki *[awaking with a start]*
Gia il sole!
[rises]
*[goes towards Butterfly and touches her
on the shoulder]*
Ciociosan...

Butterfly *[starts and says confidently]*
Verrà... verrà... col pieno sole.
*[Butterfly sees the child has fallen asleep
and takes him in her arms, turning to go
up to the next storey]*

Suzuki
Salite a riposare, affranta siete
al suo venire vi chiamerò.

Butterfly *[going up the staircase]*
Dormi amor mio,
dormi sul mio cor.

sounds from the harbour]
[The curtain rises]
*[Butterfly, still motionless, is gazing
out into the distance; the child the child
is asleep on a cushion; and Suzuki,
kneeling bent over the child, has also
fallen asleep]*
*[The first streaks of dawn appear in the
sky]*
[The rosy dawn spreads]
[The day breaks].
[The sunshine streams in from outside]
*[Butterfly at length rouses herself, and
touches Suzuki on the shoulder; the
latter
wakes with a start and rises, whilst
Butterfly turns toward the baby, and
takes him up with tender care]*

Suzuki *[awaking with a start]*
It's daylight!
[rises]
*[goes towards Butterfly and touches her
on the shoulder]*
Cio-cio-san…

Butterfly *[starts and says confidently]*
He'll come… He'll come.. this morning.
*[Butterfly sees the child has fallen asleep
and takes him in her arms, turning to go
up to the next storey]*

Suzuki
Go up and rest, you must be tired
I'll call you when he gets here.

Butterfly *[going up the staircase]*
Sleep my darling,
sleep on my heart.

Tu se con Dio
ed io col mio dolor.
A te i rai
degli astri d'or:
Bimbo mio dormi!

Suzuki *[sadly, shaking her head]*
Povera Butterfly!

Butterfly *[enters the room above]* *[voice a little farther off]*
Dormi amor mio,
dormi sul mio cor.
[voice farther off]
Tu sei con Dio
ed io col mio dolor.
[dying away in the distance]

Suzuki *[kneels before the image of Buddha]*
Povera Butterfly!
[rises and goes to open the shosi*]*
*[Light knocking at the door is heard * * *]*
Chi sia?...
*[louder knocking heaard * * * *]*
[goes to open]
[cries out in great surprise]
Oh!...

Sharpless *[on the threshold, signs to Suzuki to be quiet]*
Stz!

Pinkerton *[motions Suzuki to be silent]*
Zitta!

Suzuki
Zitta!

You're safe with God
and I with my grief.
On you still shines
the ray of the golden stars:
Sleep little darling!

Suzuki *[sadly, shaking her head]*
Poor Butterfly!

Butterfly *[enters the room above]*
[voice a little farther off]
Sleep my darling,
sleep on my heart.
[voice farther off]
You're safe with God
and I with my grief.
[dying away in the distance]

Suzuki *[kneels before the image of Buddha]*
Poor Butterfly!
[rises and goes to open the shosi*]*
*[Light knocking at the door is heard * * *]*
Who is it?...
*[louder knocking heaard * * * *]*
[goes to open]
[cries out in great surprise]
Oh!...

Sharpless *[on the threshold, signs to Suzuki to be quiet]*
Stz!

Pinkerton *[motions Suzuki to be silent]*
Hush!

Suzuki
Hush!

Pinkerton
Zitta! Zitta!
*[Pinkerton and Sharpless enter
cautiously on tip-toe]*

Pinkerton *[anxiously to Suzuki]*
Non la destar.

Suzuki
Era stanca sì tanto! Vi stette ad aspettare
tutta la notte col bimbo.

Pinkerton
Come sapea?

Suzuki
Non giunge
da tre anni una nave nel porto, che da
lunge
Butterfly non ne scruti il color, la
bandiera.

Sharpless *[to Pinkerton]*
Ve lo dissi?!...

Suzuki *[going]*
La chiamo...

Pinkerton *[stopping Suzuki]*
No non ancor.

Suzuki *[Pointing to the masses of
flowers all about the room]*
Lo vedete, ier sera,
la stanza volle sparger di fiori.

Sharpless *[touched]*
Ve lo dissi?...

Pinkerton
Hush!Quiet!
*[Pinkerton and Sharpless enter
cautiously on tip-toe]*

Pinkerton *[anxiously to Suzuki]*
Don't let her hear.

Suzuki
She was so tired! She and the baby
were waiting for you all night.

Pinkerton
How did she find out?

Suzuki
No ship
has entered the harbor in these three
years that
Butterfly has not examined its colors,
its flags.

Sharpless *[to Pinkerton]*
Didn't I tell you?!...

Suzuki *[going]*
I'll call her…

Pinkerton *[stopping Suzuki]*
No, not yet.

Suzuki *[Pointing to the masses of
flowers all about the room]*
Look around you, last night
she spread flowers around the room.

Sharpless *[touched]*
Didn't I tell you?...

Pinkerton *[troubled]*
Che pena!

Suzuki *[hears a noise in the garden, goes to look outside the* shosi *and exclaims in surprise]*
Chi c'è là fuori
nel giardino?...
Una donna!!..

Pinkerton *[goes to Suzuki and leads her down the stage again, urging her to speak in a whisper]*
Zitta!

Suzuki *[excitedly]*
Chi è? chi è?

Sharpless *[to Pinkerton]*
Meglio dirle ogni cosa...

Suzuki *[in consternation]*
Chi è? chi è?

Pinkerton *[embarrassed]*
È venuta con me.

Suzuki
Chi è? chi è?

Sharpless *[with restraint but deliberately]*
È sua moglie!

Suzuki *[stupefied, raises her arms to heaven, then falls on her knees with her face to the ground]*

Pinkerton *[troubled]*
How awful!

Suzuki *[hears a noise in the garden, goes to look outside the* shosi *and exclaims in surprise]*
Who's that outside
in the garden?...
A woman!!..

Pinkerton *[goes to Suzuki and leads her down the stage again, urging her to speak in a whisper]*
Quiet!

Suzuki *[excitedly]*
Who is she? Who is she?

Sharpless *[to Pinkerton]*
It's better to tell her the truth...

Suzuki *[in consternation]*
Who is she? Who is she?

Pinkerton *[embarrassed]*
She came with me,

Suzuki
Who is she? Who is she?

Sharpless *[with restraint but deliberately]*
She's his wife!

Suzuki *[stupefied, raises her arms to heaven, then falls on her knees with her face to the ground]*

Anime sante degli avi! Alla piccina
s'è spento il sol,
s'è spento il sol!

Sharpless [soothes Suzuki and raises her
from the ground]
Scegliemmo quest'ora mattutina
per ritrovarti sola, Suzuki, e alla gran
prova
un aiuto, un sostegno cercar con te.

Suzuki [in despair]
Che giova? che giova?

Sharpless [takes Suzuki aside and tries
to persuade her into consenting, whilst
Pinkerton getting more and more
agitated, wanders about the room,
noticing all details]
Lo so che alle sue pene
non ci sono conforti!
Ma del bimbo conviene
assicurar le sorti!

Pinkerton
Oh! l'amara fragranza
di questi fior,
velenosa al cor mi va.

Sharpless
La pietosa
che entrar non osa
materna cura
del bimbo avrà

Suzuki
Oh me trista!
E volete ch'io chieda
ad una madre...

Blessed souls of our fathers! For little
madame the sun has darkened,
the sun has darkened!

Sharpless [soothes Suzuki and raises
her from the ground]
We've chosen this early morning hour
to find you alone, Suzuki, so that you'd
give us
your help, and support.

Suzuki [in despair]
How can I? How can I?

Sharpless [takes Suzuki aside and tries
to persuade her into consenting, whilst
Pinkerton getting more and more
agitated, wanders about the room,
noticing all details]
I know that for such grief
there's no comfort!
But the child's future welfare
we must be protected.

Pinkerton
Oh! How bitter the fragrance of all
these flowers,
It's like poison to my heart.

Sharpless
This pitying woman
who dares not enter
mother's care
will provide for the child

Suzuki
Oh I'm so sad!
And do you ask me
to go and tell a mother...

Pinkerton
Immutata è la stanza
dei nostri amor...

Sharpless
Suvvia,
parla,
suvvia,
[Pinkerton goes toward the image of Buddha]
parla con quella pia
e conducila qui... s'anche la veda
Butterfly, non importa.
Anzi, meglio se accorta
del vero si facesse alla sua vista.
Suvvia, parla con quella pia,
suvvia, conducila qui,
conducila qui.

Pinkerton |
Ma un gel di morte vi sta.
[sees his own likeness]
Il mio ritratto...
Tre anni son passati,
tre anni son passati,
tre anni son passati e noverati
n'ha i giorni e l'ore,
i giorni e l'ore!

Suzuki
e volete ch'io chieda
ad una madre...
Oh! me trista!
Oh! me trista!
Anime sante degli avi!...
Alla piccina
s'è spento il sol!
Oh! me trista!
Anime sante degli avi!...

Pinkerton
I see nothing has changed here where
once we loved…

Sharpless
Please,
tell me,
please,
[Pinkerton goes toward the image of Buddha]
Go and speak with that gentle lady
Bring her here… even if Butterfly sees
her, it doesn't matter.
Even better if she realizes
with her eyes the truth.
Come, speak with that gentle lady
come, bring her here,
bring her here.

Pinkerton
But a deathly fragrance plagues the air.
[sees his own likeness]
My portrait…
Three years have gone,
Three years have gone,
Three years have gone and she counted
every day and every hour,
every day and every hour!

Suzuki
And do you ask me
to go and tell a mother…
Oh! I'm so sad!
Oh! I'm so sad!
Blessed souls of our fathers!
To the little madame
the sun has darkened!
Oh! I'm so sad!
Blessed souls of our fathers!

MADAMA BUTTERFLY (ENGLISH AND ITALIAN EDITION)

Alla piccina
s'è spento il sol!
[Sharpless pushes her into the garden to join Mrs. Pinkerton]

Sharpless
Vien, Suzuki, vien!

Pinkerton [overcome by emotion and unable to restrain his tears, approaching Sharpless and says to him resolutely]
Non posso rimaner;

Suzuki [going away]
Oh! me trista!

Pinkerton
Sharpless, v'aspetto
per via...

Sharpless
Non ve l'avevo detto?

Pinkerton [giving Sharpless some money]
Datele voi qualche soccorso...
mi struggo dal rimorso,
mi struggo dal rimorso.

Sharpless
Vel dissi? vi ricorda?
quando la man vi diede:
``badate! Ella ci crede''
e fui profeta allor!
Sorda ai consigli,
sorda ai dubbî, vilipesa
nell'ostinata attesa
raccolse il cor...

To the little madame
the sun has darkened!
[Sharpless pushes her into the garden to join Mrs. Pinkerton]

Sharpless
Come, Suzuki, come!

Pinkerton [overcome by emotion and unable to restrain his tears, approaching Sharpless and says to him resolutely]
I can't stay.

Suzuki [going away]
Oh!I'm so sad!

Pinkerton
Sharpless, I'll wait for you
by the roadside...

Sharpless
Didn't I tell you?

Pinkerton [giving Sharpless some money]
Give her some assistance...
I'm devastated by remorse,
I'm devastated by remorse.

Sharpless
I told you? You remember?
When she gave you her hand:
"Be careful! She trusts you"
I was a prophet!
But she didn't listen to my advice,
my doubts, blindly thinking to your
return she collected strenght
in her heart...

Pinkerton
Sì, tutto in un istante
io vedo il fallo mio e sento
che di questo tormento
tregua mai non avrò,
mai non avrò! no!

Sharpless
Andate: il triste vero
da sola apprenderà.

Pinkerton *[softly lamenting]*
Addio fiorito asil
di letizia e d'amor...
Sempre il mite suo sembiante
con strazio atroce vedrò...

Sharpless
Ma or quel cor sincero
pressago è già...

Pinkerton
Addio fiorito asil...

Sharpless
Vel dissi... vi ricorda?...
e fui profeta allor.

Pinkerton
Non reggo al tuo squallor,
ah! non reggo al tuo squallor!
Fuggo, fuggo, son vil!
Addio, non reggo al tuo squallor,

Sharpless
Andate, il triste vero
apprenderà.

Pinkerton
Yes, all of sudden I see
I was mistaken and I feel
that from this agony
I will never free myself
I will never! Never!

Sharpless
Now leave: she will learn of the
cruel truth alone.

Pinkerton *[softly lamenting]*
Goodbye flowered home
home of joy and love…
I'll be obsessed forever by
all she suffered because of me.

Sharpless
But now this sincere heart
might already know…

Pinkerton
Goodbye, flowered home…

Sharpless
I told you… You remember?...
I was a prophet.

Pinkerton
I can not bear your squalor,
ah! I can not bear your squalor!
I flee, I flee, like a coward!
Goodbye, I can not bear your squalor,

Sharpless
Then leave, the truth she'll have to find
out all by herself.

Pinkerton
ah! non reggo, son vil!
[wrings the Consul's hand, and goes out quickly by the door on the right: Sharpless bows his head sadly]
[Kate and Suzuki come from the garden]

Kate *[gently to Suzuki]*
Glielo dirai?

Suzuki
Prometto.

Kate
E le darai consiglio
d'affidarmi?...

Suzuki
Prometto.

Kate
Lo terrò come un figlio.
Suzuki
Vi credo. Ma bisogna ch'io le sia sola
accanto...
Nella grande ora... sola! Piangerà tanto
tanto!
piangerà tanto!

Butterfly *[voice from afar, calling from the room above]*
Suzuki!
[nearer] Suzuki!
Dove sei?
Suzuki!
[appears at the head of the staircase]

Suzuki
Son qui... pregavo e rimettevo a posto...

Pinkerton
ah! I can not stay, I'm a coward!
[wrings the Consul's hand, and goes out quickly by the door on the right: Sharpless bows his head sadly]
[Kate and Suzuki come from the garden]

Kate *[gently to Suzuki]*
You're going to tell her?

Suzuki
I promise.

Kate
And will you advise her to
entrust me?...

Suzuki
I promise.

Kate
I will treat him like a son.

Suzuki
I trust you. But I must be the only one on
her side...
In that awful moment... Alone! She will
cry so much!
She will cry so much!

Butterfly*[voice from afar, calling from the room above]*
Suzuki!
[nearer] Suzuki!
Where are you?
Suzuki!
[appears at the head of the staircase]

Suzuki
I'm here... I was praying and making

[Butterfly begins to come down stairs]
No...
[rushes toward the staircase to prevent Butterfly from coming down]
no... no... no... no... non scendete...
[Butterfly comes down quickly, freeing herself from Suzuki who tries in vain to hold her back]
[crying out] no... no... no...

Butterfly *[pacing the room in great, but joyful excitement]*
È qui,... è qui... dove è nascosto?
è qui,... è qui...
[catching sight of Sharpless]
Ecco il Console...
[In alarm, looking for Pinkerton]
e... dove?... dove?...
[Butterfly, after having searched in every corner, in the little recess and behind the screen, looks around in anguish]

Non c'è!..
[sees Kate and looks at her fixedly]
[to Kate] Chi siete?
Perchè veniste?
Niuno parla!...
Perché piangete?
[is afraid of understanding and shrinks together like a frightened child]
No, non ditemi nulla... nulla... forse potrei
cader morta sull'attimo...
[with affectionate and childlike kindness to Suzuki]
Tu Suzuki che sei
tanto buona, non piangere! e mi vuoi tanto bene

sure we're ready...
[Butterfly begins to come down stairs]
No...
[rushes toward the staircase to prevent Butterfly from coming down]
no... no... no... no... Don't come down...
[Butterfly comes down quickly, freeing herself from Suzuki who tries in vain to hold her back]
*[crying out]*no... no... no...

Butterfly*[pacing the room in great, but joyful excitement]*
He's here,... He's here... Where is hiding?
He's here,... He's here...
[catching sight of Sharpless]
Here's the Consul...
[In alarm, looking for Pinkerton]
And where is he?... Where is he?
[Butterfly, after having searched in every corner, in the little recess and behind the screen, looks around in anguish]
He's not here!..
[sees Kate and looks at her fixedly]
[to Kate] Who are you?
Why have you come here?
No one answers!...
Why are you crying?
[is afraid of understanding and shrinks together like a frightened child]
No, don't say a word now... Nothing... I think
I'd die the moment I hear it...
[with affectionate and childlike kindness to Suzuki]
You Suzuki, who are always
so good, don't cry for me! Since you love me so

un Sì, un No, di' piano...
Vive?

Suzuki
Sì.

Butterfly [transfixed; as though she had received a mortal blow]
Ma non viene
più. Te l'han detto!...
[Suzuki is silent]
[angered at Suzuki's silence]
Vespa! Voglio che tu risponda.

Suzuki
Mai più.

Butterfly [coldly]
Ma è giunto ieri?

Suzuki
Sì.
[Butterfly, who has understood, looks at Kate as though fascinated]

Butterfly
Quella donna bionda
mi fa tanta paura! tanta paura!

Kate [simply]
Son la causa innocente
d'ogni vostra sciagura.
Perdonatemi.
[about to approach Butterfly who motions her to keep away]

Butterfly
Non mi toccate.
[in a calm voice]

dearly, just whisper "yes" or "no"... Is he alive?

Suzuki
Yes.

Butterfly[transfixed; as though she had received a mortal blow]
But he won't come back.
They've told you!...
[Suzuki is silent]
[angered at Suzuki's silence]
Wasp! I want you to answer.

Suzuki
Never again.

Butterfly[coldly]
But he arrived yesterday?

Suzuki
Yes.
[Butterfly, who has understood, looks at Kate as though fascinated]

Butterfly
That blonde woman makes me feel
very frightened! So terribly frightened!

Kate[simply]
I'm the innocent cause
of your disgrace.
Forgive me.
[about to approach Butterfly who motions her to keep away]

Butterfly
Do not touch me.
[in a calm voice]

Quanto
tempo è che v'ha sposata... voi?

Kate
Un anno.
[shyly] E non mi lascierete far nulla pel
bambino?
[Butterfly is silent]
Lo terrei con cura affetuosa...
[Butterfly does not reply]
*[impressed by Butterfly's silence, and
deeply moved, persists]*
È triste cosa, triste cosa,
ma fatelo pel suo meglio.

Butterfly *[remains motionless]*
Chissà!
Tutto è compiuto ormai!

Kate *[coaxingly]*
Potete perdonarmi, Butterfly?

Butterfly *[solemnly]*
Sotto il gran ponte del cielo non v'è
donna di voi più felice.
[passionately]
Siatelo sempre,
non v'attristate per me...
Mi piacerebbe pur che gli diceste
che pace io troverò.

Kate *[holding out her hand]*
La man,... la man, me la dareste?

Butterfly *[decidedly but kindly]*
Vi prego, questo... no...
Andate adesso.

How long ago
has he married... you?

Kate
A year.
[shyly] And won't you let me do
something for the baby?
[Butterfly is silent]
I will take care of him dearly…
[Butterfly does not reply]
*[impressed by Butterfly's silence, and
deeply moved, persists]*
I know it's such a sad moment for you
but do this for his good.

Butterfly *[remains motionless]*
Who knows!
All is done now!

Kate *[coaxingly]*
Can you forgive me, Butterfly?

Butterfly *[solemnly]*
Beneath the great arch of heaven
there is no woman as happy as you are.
[passionately]
Always be happy,
and don't be sad for me…
I'd be pleased that you should
tell him that I'll find peace.

Kate *[holding out her hand]*
Your hand… Your hand, may I take it?

Butterfly *[decidedly but kindly]*
Please don't.. no…
Now leave me.

Kate *[going towards Sharpless]*
Povera piccina!

Sharpless *[deeply moved]*
È un immensa pietà!

Kate
E il figlio lo darà?

Butterfly *[who has heard, says solemnly]*
A lui lo potrò dare
se lo verrà a cercare.
[with marked meaning, but quite simply]
Fra mezz'ora salite la collina.
[Suzuki escorts Kate and Sharpless who go out by the door on the right]
[Butterfly is on the point of collapsing. Suzuki hastens to support her and leads her to the middle of the stage]

Suzuki *[placing her hand on Butterfly's heart]*
Come una mosca prigioniera
l'ali batte il piccolo cuor!
[Butterfly gradually recovers; seeing that it is broad daylight she disengages herself from Suzuki and says to her]

Butterfly
Troppa luce è di fuor,
e troppa primavera.
[pointing to the windows]
Chiudi.
[Suzuki goes to shut the doors and curtains, so that the room is almost in total darkness]
[Suzuki returns towards Butterfly]

Kate *[going towards Sharpless]*
Poor little woman!

Sharpless *[deeply moved]*
It's such a shame!

Kate
And will you give him his son?

Butterfly *[who has heard, says solemnly]*
I will give him his son
if he comes to fetch him.
[with marked meaning, but quite simply]
In half an hour he can climb this hill.
[Suzuki escorts Kate and Sharpless who go out by the door on the right]
[Butterfly is on the point of collapsing. Suzuki hastens to support her and leads her to the middle of the stage]

Suzuki *[placing her hand on Butterfly's heart]*
Like the wings of an imprisoned fly
her little heart is beating!
[Butterfly gradually recovers; seeing that it is broad daylight she disengages herself from Suzuki and says to her]

Butterfly
It's too bright outside,
and too much spring.
[pointing to the windows]
Close them.
[Suzuki goes to shut the doors and curtains, so that the room is almost in total darkness]
[Suzuki returns towards Butterfly]

Butterfly
Il bimbo ove sia?

Suzuki
Giuoca... Lo chiamo?

Butterfly
Lascialo giuocar, lascialo giuocar...
Va a fargli compagnia.
[Suzuki refuses to go away and throws herself weeping at Butterfly's feet]

Suzuki
Non vi voglio lasciar.
No! no! no! no!

Butterfly
Sai la canzone?
``Varcò le chiuse porte,
prese il posto di tutto, se n'andò
e nulla vi lasciò,
nulla, nulla, fuor che la morte."

Suzuki *[weeping]*
Resto con voi.

Butterfly *[with decision clapping her hands loudly]*
Va, va. Te lo comando.
[Makes Suzuki, who is weeping bitterly, rise, and pushes her outside the exit on the left]
[Suzuki's sobs are heard]
[Butterfly lights the lamp in front of Buddha]
[she bows down]
Butterfly remains motionless, lost in sorrowful thought. Suzuki's sobs are still heard, they die away by degrees.

Butterfly
Where is the baby?

Suzuki
He's playing… Shall I fetch him?

Butterfly
Let him play, let him play…
Go and keep him company.
[Suzuki refuses to go away and throws herself weeping at Butterfly's feet]

Suzuki
I won't leave you alone.
No! no! no! no!

Butterfly
Do you know the song?
"He entered through closed gates,
he replaced everything, then he went
and nothing was left to us,
nothing, nothing, but death."

Suzuki *[weeping]*
I'll stay with you.

Butterfly *[with decision clapping her hands loudly]*
Go, go. I command you.
[Makes Suzuki, who is weeping bitterly, rise, and pushes her outside the exit on the left]
[Suzuki's sobs are heard]
[Butterfly lights the lamp in front of Buddha]
[she bows down]
Butterfly remains motionless, lost in sorrowful thought. Suzuki's sobs are still heard, they die away by degrees.

Butterfly has a convulsive movement.
Butterfly goes toward the shrine and lifts
the white veil from it; throws this across
the screen; then takes the dagger, which,
enclosed in a waxen case, is leaning
against the wall near the image of
Buddha.
Butterfly piously kisses the blade,
holding it by the point and the handle
with both hands.

Butterfly *[softly reading the words*
inscribed on it]
Con onor muore
chi non può serbar vita con onore.
[points the knife sideways at her throat]
[The door on the left opens, showing
Suzuki's arm pushing the child towards
his mother: he runs in with outstretched
hands. Butterfly lets the dagger fall,
darts toward the baby, and hugs and
kisses him almost to suffocation]

Butterfly
Tu? tu? tu? tu? tu? tu? tu?
piccolo Iddio!
Amore, amore mio,
fior di giglio e di rosa.
[taking the child's head in her hands, she
draws it to her]
Non saperlo mai
per te, pei tuoi puri
occhi, muor Butterfly
perché tu possa andar
di là dal mare
senza che ti rimorda ai dì maturi
il materno abbandono.
[exaltedly]
O a me, sceso dal trono

Butterfly has a convulsive movement.
Butterfly goes toward the shrine and lifts
the white veil from it; throws this across
the screen; then takes the dagger, which,
enclosed in a waxen case, is leaning
against the wall near the image of
Buddha.
Butterfly piously kisses the blade,
holding it by the point and the handle
with both hands.

Butterfly *[softly reading the words*
inscribed on it]
Death with honor
is better than a life filled with dishonor.
[points the knife sideways at her throat]
[The door on the left opens, showing
Suzuki's arm pushing the child towards
his mother: he runs in with outstretched
hands. Butterfly lets the dagger fall,
darts toward the baby, and hugs and
kisses him almost to suffocation]

Butterfly
You? You? You? You? You? You?
Little God!
My love, my darling,
flower of lily and rose.
[taking the child's head in her hands, she
draws it to her]
You must never know
it's for you, for your pure
eyes, that Butterfly must die
so you can sail away
across the ocean
and never know the sadness when are
older of a mother who abandoned you.
[exaltedly]
My son, sent to me from

dell'alto Paradiso,
guarda ben fiso, fiso
di tua madre la faccia!...
che te'n resti una traccia,
guarda ben!
Amore, addio! addio! piccolo amor!
Va. Gioca, gioca.

Butterfly takes the child, seats him on a stool with his face turned to the left, gives him the American flag and a doll and urges him to play with them, while she gently bandages his eyes. Then she seizes the dagger, and with her eyes still fixed on the child, goes behind the screen.

The knife is heard falling to the ground, and the large white veil disappears behind the screen.

Butterfly is seen emerging from behind the screen; tottering, she gropes her way toward the child. The large white veil is round her neck; smiling feebly she greets the child with her hand and drags herself up to him. She has just enough strength left to embrace him, then falls to the ground beside him.

Pinkerton *[within] [calling]*
Butterfly! Butterfly! Butterfly!

The door on the right opens violently - Pinkerton and Sharpless rush into the room and up to Butterfly, who with a feeble gesture points to the child and dies. Pinkerton falls on his knees, whilst Sharpless takes the child and kisses him, sobbing.

Curtain descends swiftly

---

the highest Paradise,
look well, very well
your mother's face!...
so that a trace may remain,
look carefully!
My darling, goodbye! Goodbye! My sweet child! Now go. Play, play.

Butterfly takes the child, seats him on a stool with his face turned to the left, gives him the American flag and a doll and urges him to play with them, while she gently bandages his eyes. Then she seizes the dagger, and with her eyes still fixed on the child, goes behind the screen.

The knife is heard falling to the ground, and the large white veil disappears behind the screen.

Butterfly is seen emerging from behind the screen; tottering, she gropes her way toward the child. The large white veil is round her neck; smiling feebly she greets the child with her hand and drags herself up to him. She has just enough strength left to embrace him, then falls to the ground beside him.

Pinkerton *[within] [calling]*
Butterfly! Butterfly! Butterfly!

The door on the right opens violently - Pinkerton and Sharpless rush into the room and up to Butterfly, who with a feeble gesture points to the child and dies. Pinkerton falls on his knees, whilst Sharpless takes the child and kisses him, sobbing.

Curtain descends swiftly

Printed in the USA
CPSIA information can be obtained
at www.ICGtesting.com
LVHW070347020124
767819LV00006B/776